Proper Education Group

4 Practice Tests for the North Carolina Real Estate Exam

"The secret to getting ahead is getting started."
Mark Twain

Table of Contents

Introduction

1.1 Requirements

On the day of the test, you must bring the following:

1. **TWO** forms of valid and non-expired government-issued ID with a valid signature. One must be government issued and include a photo. Examples include:
   a. Driver's license
   b. State issued identification (ex. non-driver ID)
   c. United States Passport
   d. Credit card
2. A second ID that contains your signature and legal name
3. A basic non-scientific calculator

You are not required to bring a calculator, but you are **highly encouraged to do so** as there will be simple mathematical questions that require multiplication and division. Do not rely on the one on your phone because **phones will not be allowed**.

1.2 About the Exam

The test is 4 hours long and composed of two sections.

The national portion is composed of 100 multiple choice questions. You must answer at least 71 questions of the national portion correctly to pass.

The state portion is composed of 40 multiple choice questions. You must answer at least 29 questions of the state portion correctly to pass.

The exam is administered through a computer.

1.3 How to Apply

To apply for the exam, visit the website below and submit the required the forms:

https://www.ncrec.gov/Brochures/general.pdf

All of the official documentation pertaining payments, documents, and forms can be found there.

1.4 Exam Results

Your score will be given to you immediately after finishing the exam.

Practice Test 1

Directions:

1.   You have a 4-hour time limit to complete the whole exam.

2.   To pass, you must answer at least 71 out of 100 questions correctly on the national portion **AND** at least 29 out of 40 questions on the state portion.

3.   Some questions will require mathematics. You may use a calculator.

4.   **Phones and pagers are not allowed. Having either will result in automatic dismissal from the exam and nullification of exam scores.**

Tips:

- Answer all questions even if you are unsure.
- Mark any questions you are stuck on and revisit them after you are done. The exam is timed so make sure you finish as many questions as you can.
- After reading the question, try answering it in your head first to avoid getting confused by the choices.
- Read the entire question before looking at the answers.
- Use the process of elimination to filter out choices that don't seem correct to increase your chances of selecting the correct answer.
- Be aware of important keywords like **not, sometimes, always,** and **never**. These words completely alter the ask of the question so it's important to keep track of them.

PLEASE READ THESE INSTRUCTIONS CAREFULLY.

Name: _____   Date: _____

NATIONAL PORTION

1.	Ⓐ Ⓑ Ⓒ Ⓓ	31.	Ⓐ Ⓑ Ⓒ Ⓓ	61.	Ⓐ Ⓑ Ⓒ Ⓓ	91.	Ⓐ Ⓑ Ⓒ Ⓓ
2.	Ⓐ Ⓑ Ⓒ Ⓓ	32.	Ⓐ Ⓑ Ⓒ Ⓓ	62.	Ⓐ Ⓑ Ⓒ Ⓓ	92.	Ⓐ Ⓑ Ⓒ Ⓓ
3.	Ⓐ Ⓑ Ⓒ Ⓓ	33.	Ⓐ Ⓑ Ⓒ Ⓓ	63.	Ⓐ Ⓑ Ⓒ Ⓓ	93.	Ⓐ Ⓑ Ⓒ Ⓓ
4.	Ⓐ Ⓑ Ⓒ Ⓓ	34.	Ⓐ Ⓑ Ⓒ Ⓓ	64.	Ⓐ Ⓑ Ⓒ Ⓓ	94.	Ⓐ Ⓑ Ⓒ Ⓓ
5.	Ⓐ Ⓑ Ⓒ Ⓓ	35.	Ⓐ Ⓑ Ⓒ Ⓓ	65.	Ⓐ Ⓑ Ⓒ Ⓓ	95.	Ⓐ Ⓑ Ⓒ Ⓓ
6.	Ⓐ Ⓑ Ⓒ Ⓓ	36.	Ⓐ Ⓑ Ⓒ Ⓓ	66.	Ⓐ Ⓑ Ⓒ Ⓓ	96.	Ⓐ Ⓑ Ⓒ Ⓓ
7.	Ⓐ Ⓑ Ⓒ Ⓓ	37.	Ⓐ Ⓑ Ⓒ Ⓓ	67.	Ⓐ Ⓑ Ⓒ Ⓓ	97.	Ⓐ Ⓑ Ⓒ Ⓓ
8.	Ⓐ Ⓑ Ⓒ Ⓓ	38.	Ⓐ Ⓑ Ⓒ Ⓓ	68.	Ⓐ Ⓑ Ⓒ Ⓓ	98.	Ⓐ Ⓑ Ⓒ Ⓓ
9.	Ⓐ Ⓑ Ⓒ Ⓓ	39.	Ⓐ Ⓑ Ⓒ Ⓓ	69.	Ⓐ Ⓑ Ⓒ Ⓓ	99.	Ⓐ Ⓑ Ⓒ Ⓓ
10.	Ⓐ Ⓑ Ⓒ Ⓓ	40.	Ⓐ Ⓑ Ⓒ Ⓓ	70.	Ⓐ Ⓑ Ⓒ Ⓓ	100.	Ⓐ Ⓑ Ⓒ Ⓓ
11.	Ⓐ Ⓑ Ⓒ Ⓓ	41.	Ⓐ Ⓑ Ⓒ Ⓓ	71.	Ⓐ Ⓑ Ⓒ Ⓓ		
12.	Ⓐ Ⓑ Ⓒ Ⓓ	42.	Ⓐ Ⓑ Ⓒ Ⓓ	72.	Ⓐ Ⓑ Ⓒ Ⓓ		
13.	Ⓐ Ⓑ Ⓒ Ⓓ	43.	Ⓐ Ⓑ Ⓒ Ⓓ	73.	Ⓐ Ⓑ Ⓒ Ⓓ		
14.	Ⓐ Ⓑ Ⓒ Ⓓ	44.	Ⓐ Ⓑ Ⓒ Ⓓ	74.	Ⓐ Ⓑ Ⓒ Ⓓ		
15.	Ⓐ Ⓑ Ⓒ Ⓓ	45.	Ⓐ Ⓑ Ⓒ Ⓓ	75.	Ⓐ Ⓑ Ⓒ Ⓓ		
16.	Ⓐ Ⓑ Ⓒ Ⓓ	46.	Ⓐ Ⓑ Ⓒ Ⓓ	76.	Ⓐ Ⓑ Ⓒ Ⓓ		
17	Ⓐ Ⓑ Ⓒ Ⓓ	47.	Ⓐ Ⓑ Ⓒ Ⓓ	77.	Ⓐ Ⓑ Ⓒ Ⓓ		
18.	Ⓐ Ⓑ Ⓒ Ⓓ	48.	Ⓐ Ⓑ Ⓒ Ⓓ	78.	Ⓐ Ⓑ Ⓒ Ⓓ		
19.	Ⓐ Ⓑ Ⓒ Ⓓ	49.	Ⓐ Ⓑ Ⓒ Ⓓ	79.	Ⓐ Ⓑ Ⓒ Ⓓ		
20.	Ⓐ Ⓑ Ⓒ Ⓓ	50.	Ⓐ Ⓑ Ⓒ Ⓓ	80.	Ⓐ Ⓑ Ⓒ Ⓓ		
21.	Ⓐ Ⓑ Ⓒ Ⓓ	51.	Ⓐ Ⓑ Ⓒ Ⓓ	81.	Ⓐ Ⓑ Ⓒ Ⓓ		
22.	Ⓐ Ⓑ Ⓒ Ⓓ	52.	Ⓐ Ⓑ Ⓒ Ⓓ	82.	Ⓐ Ⓑ Ⓒ Ⓓ		
23.	Ⓐ Ⓑ Ⓒ Ⓓ	53.	Ⓐ Ⓑ Ⓒ Ⓓ	83.	Ⓐ Ⓑ Ⓒ Ⓓ		
24.	Ⓐ Ⓑ Ⓒ Ⓓ	54.	Ⓐ Ⓑ Ⓒ Ⓓ	84.	Ⓐ Ⓑ Ⓒ Ⓓ		
25.	Ⓐ Ⓑ Ⓒ Ⓓ	55.	Ⓐ Ⓑ Ⓒ Ⓓ	85.	Ⓐ Ⓑ Ⓒ Ⓓ		
26.	Ⓐ Ⓑ Ⓒ Ⓓ	56.	Ⓐ Ⓑ Ⓒ Ⓓ	86.	Ⓐ Ⓑ Ⓒ Ⓓ		
27.	Ⓐ Ⓑ Ⓒ Ⓓ	57.	Ⓐ Ⓑ Ⓒ Ⓓ	87.	Ⓐ Ⓑ Ⓒ Ⓓ		
28.	Ⓐ Ⓑ Ⓒ Ⓓ	58.	Ⓐ Ⓑ Ⓒ Ⓓ	88.	Ⓐ Ⓑ Ⓒ Ⓓ		
29.	Ⓐ Ⓑ Ⓒ Ⓓ	59.	Ⓐ Ⓑ Ⓒ Ⓓ	89.	Ⓐ Ⓑ Ⓒ Ⓓ		
30.	Ⓐ Ⓑ Ⓒ Ⓓ	60.	Ⓐ Ⓑ Ⓒ Ⓓ	90.	Ⓐ Ⓑ Ⓒ Ⓓ		

Practice Test 1

Name: _____   Date: _____

STATE PORTION

#						#				
1.	Ⓐ	Ⓑ	Ⓒ	Ⓓ		31.	Ⓐ	Ⓑ	Ⓒ	Ⓓ
2.	Ⓐ	Ⓑ	Ⓒ	Ⓓ		32.	Ⓐ	Ⓑ	Ⓒ	Ⓓ
3.	Ⓐ	Ⓑ	Ⓒ	Ⓓ		33.	Ⓐ	Ⓑ	Ⓒ	Ⓓ
4.	Ⓐ	Ⓑ	Ⓒ	Ⓓ		34.	Ⓐ	Ⓑ	Ⓒ	Ⓓ
5.	Ⓐ	Ⓑ	Ⓒ	Ⓓ		35.	Ⓐ	Ⓑ	Ⓒ	Ⓓ
6.	Ⓐ	Ⓑ	Ⓒ	Ⓓ		36.	Ⓐ	Ⓑ	Ⓒ	Ⓓ
7.	Ⓐ	Ⓑ	Ⓒ	Ⓓ		37.	Ⓐ	Ⓑ	Ⓒ	Ⓓ
8.	Ⓐ	Ⓑ	Ⓒ	Ⓓ		38.	Ⓐ	Ⓑ	Ⓒ	Ⓓ
9.	Ⓐ	Ⓑ	Ⓒ	Ⓓ		39.	Ⓐ	Ⓑ	Ⓒ	Ⓓ
10.	Ⓐ	Ⓑ	Ⓒ	Ⓓ		40.	Ⓐ	Ⓑ	Ⓒ	Ⓓ
11.	Ⓐ	Ⓑ	Ⓒ	Ⓓ						
12.	Ⓐ	Ⓑ	Ⓒ	Ⓓ						
13.	Ⓐ	Ⓑ	Ⓒ	Ⓓ						
14.	Ⓐ	Ⓑ	Ⓒ	Ⓓ						
15.	Ⓐ	Ⓑ	Ⓒ	Ⓓ						
16.	Ⓐ	Ⓑ	Ⓒ	Ⓓ						
17	Ⓐ	Ⓑ	Ⓒ	Ⓓ						
18.	Ⓐ	Ⓑ	Ⓒ	Ⓓ						
19.	Ⓐ	Ⓑ	Ⓒ	Ⓓ						
20.	Ⓐ	Ⓑ	Ⓒ	Ⓓ						
21.	Ⓐ	Ⓑ	Ⓒ	Ⓓ						
22.	Ⓐ	Ⓑ	Ⓒ	Ⓓ						
23.	Ⓐ	Ⓑ	Ⓒ	Ⓓ						
24.	Ⓐ	Ⓑ	Ⓒ	Ⓓ						
25.	Ⓐ	Ⓑ	Ⓒ	Ⓓ						
26.	Ⓐ	Ⓑ	Ⓒ	Ⓓ						
27.	Ⓐ	Ⓑ	Ⓒ	Ⓓ						
28.	Ⓐ	Ⓑ	Ⓒ	Ⓓ						
29.	Ⓐ	Ⓑ	Ⓒ	Ⓓ						
30.	Ⓐ	Ⓑ	Ⓒ	Ⓓ						

National Portion

1. When applying for a loan, what is a **fixed rate**?

    A. A loan that has a predetermined repayment interest rate
    B. A loan whose interest rates do not change throughout the life of the loan
    C. A loan that accrues no interest
    D. A loan that pays off the interest before the principal

2. What act prohibits discrimination based on race or color?

    A. Fair Housing Act
    B. Civil Rights Act of 1866
    C. Civil Right Act of 1964
    D. Civil Rights Act Amendment of 1974

3. What is the financial document that contains a written promise to fulfill a certain payment?

    A. Invoice
    B. Promissory note
    C. Pro forma statement
    D. IOU

4. What is the term used to describe the act of replacing an existing mortgage with another?

    A. Refinancing
    B. Defaulting
    C. Foreclosure
    D. Reinvesting

5. Which is **not** an appurtenant right?

    A. Furnace
    B. Swimming pool
    C. Air conditioning
    D. All of the above

6. What is the name given to the banking option that allows a customer to deposit a specified amount for a predetermined period of time?

    A. Certificate of occupation
    B. Certificate of deposit
    C. Investment clause
    D. Mortgage

7. If a seller nets $225,000 after paying a 10% fee, what was the total he received?

    A. $202,500
    B. $224,990
    C. $250,000
    D. None of the above

8. What is the name given to the rate earned for borrowing or an investment per year?

    A. Rate lock
    B. Fixed rate
    C. Floating rate
    D. Annual percentage rate

9. Other than buying a home using traditional channels, what other methods can a prospective owner use to buy a home?

   A. Public auctions
   B. Tender
   C. Lease
   D. Escalation clause

10. What is the reviewing of a borrower's credit worthiness prior to loan approval?

   A. Buydown
   B. Pre-qualification
   C. Credit score
   D. Under qualification

11. What is the document that is used to transfer legal rights to act in the interest of a person?

   A. Disclosure form
   B. Power of attorney
   C. Pro forma statement
   D. Deed

12. What type of listing only guarantees commission for a sale within a specified period?

   A. Exclusive listing
   B. Net listing
   C. Single agency listing
   D. Multi agency listing

13. What type of brokerage mandates that the broker acts in the best interest of the buyer?

   A. Single agency
   B. Dual agency
   C. Multi agency
   D. Full service

14. What is the name of a transaction where both the buyer and seller are seeking the best deal?

   A. Real estate transaction
   B. Credit transaction
   C. Arms-length transaction
   D. Debited transaction

15. What is the name given to modification of billing calculation dates?

   A. Modified date
   B. Closing date
   C. Opening date
   D. Adjustment date

16. What is the name of the mortgage that is transferred by the seller to the buyer?

   A. Assumable mortgage
   B. Adjusted rate mortgage
   C. Fixed rate mortgage
   D. Floating mortgage

17. What is the contract that secures a future transaction?

A. Deed
B. Call option
C. Title
D. None of the above

18. What does an exclusive listing contract need to be considered valid?

A. A net listing
B. A commission rate of at least 6%
C. A specified expiration date
D. The signature of the grantee

19. What is it when another state recognizes your real estate license?

A. Transfer
B. Limited basis policy
C. Reciprocity
D. None of the above

20. Which of the following is **not** a fiduciary duty?

A. Accounting
B. Confidentiality
C. Obedience
D. Privacy

21. What are contingencies as used in real estate?

A. Conditions that must be met by both the buyer and the seller before closing
B. Conditions set by the government on buying a home
C. Conditions set by the bank in order to approve a loan for a mortgage
D. Conditions that must be met to avoid judicial foreclosure

22. Who is a co-borrower?

A. Any individual whose name appears on the loan document
B. Someone that borrows money at the same time with you
C. The mortgage broker that originates the loan for you
D. An individual that guarantees your loan

23. What is the name given to a loan taken out to finance construction?

A. Mortgage
B. Construction loan
C. Business loan
D. Personal loan

24. What is the name given to the inspection done by the buyer before closing?

A. Final inspection
B. Advertorial
C. Housing ratio
D. Final walkthrough

25. What is the name given to a mortgage whose interest rate does **not** change throughout the payment period?

    A. Adjustable mortgage rate
    B. Floating rate
    C. Fixed mortgage rate
    D. Bridge loan

26. What is defined as the percentage owned by the buyer after making a down payment?

    A. Housing ratio
    B. Debt to income ratio
    C. Loan to value ratio
    D. Floating rate

27. What is the cash-on-cash return of a $60,000 investment that generates $1,000 in monthly cash flow?

    A. 1.67%
    B. 2%
    C. 20%
    D. None of the above

28. What is the term used to refer to the responsibility one individual has for the acts of another?

    A. Vicarious liability
    B. Fixed liability
    C. Current liability
    D. Contingent

29. What is the name given to a form used to explain the role of an agent in a real estate transaction?

    A. Purchase agreement
    B. Accountability
    C. Assignment contract
    D. Agency disclosure statement

30. A number of brokers agreed on a set standard commission. What antitrust law are they guilty of violating?

    A. Commingling
    B. Price fixing
    C. Steering
    D. Discussing

31. Which government agency is responsible for determining the status of an independent contractor?

    A. Federal government
    B. Bank
    C. Department of State
    D. IRS

32. What is the nature of the title issued in condo ownership?

    A. Freehold
    B. Regular
    C. Deed
    D. Clear title

33. Mr. and Mrs. Johnson made a $350,000 profit on the sale of their primary home. How much do they owe in capital gains tax?

    A. $0
    B. $3,500
    C. $50,000
    D. Half of the amount earned

34. What is the status of an agent's license once it is revoked?

    A. Pending
    B. Cancelled
    C. Breached
    D. Suspended

35. Which insurance policy provides extra liability coverage for the insured party?

    A. Umbrella policy
    B. Home insurance
    C. Flood insurance
    D. Hazard insurance

36. What is never included in the process of valuation?

    A. Comparative Market Analysis
    B. Appraisal
    C. Location
    D. Condition of the house

37. What type of contract allows the parties involved to disaffirm without liability?

    A. Bilateral contract
    B. Implied contract
    C. Unilateral contract
    D. Voidable Contract

38. What fiduciary duty does a broker neglect by failing to disclosing the buyer's inability to afford a down payment?

    A. Obedience
    B. Disclosure
    C. Accountability
    D. Confidentiality

39. James and Peter co-own a property where they both have equal undivided interests and right of survivorship. What co-ownership agreement do they have?

    A. Tenancy in entirety
    B. Joint tenancy
    C. Tenancy in common
    D. Tenancy at will

40. What is an exclusive term to describe the lease entered when an individual buys shares from a housing corporation?

    A. Percentage lease
    B. Gross lease
    C. Net lease
    D. Proprietary lease

41. What is the state of having no legal effect?

    A. Enforceable
    B. Cancelled
    C. Void
    D. Terminated

42. How many square feet constitute an acre?

    A. 25,235
    B. 43,560
    C. 50,525
    D. 70,000

43. What is the set minimum amp for a new construction?

    A. 100 amps
    B. 150 amps
    C. 200 amps
    D. 250 amps

44. What is the debt-to-equity ratio on a mortgage valued at $1,000,000 with a loan of $750,000?

    A. 25%
    B. 50%
    C. 65%
    D. 75%

45. Who controls flood insurance?

    A. FEMA
    B. EPA
    C. CERCLA
    D. FHA

46. What is a detailed building plan that is needed before starting construction?

    A. Building design
    B. Execution plan
    C. Blueprint
    D. Authorized plan

47. What type of house insulation was banned due to the release of formaldehyde fumes?

    A. Foam boards
    B. Loose fill
    C. Vapor barriers
    D. UFFI

48. What is the term used to describe a scenario where an agent represents both the buyer and the seller?

    A. Single agency
    B. Dual agency
    C. Multi agency
    D. Representing both agency

49. Which formal agreement gives an agent the sole right to sell a property?

 A.   Purchase agreement
 B.   Floating rate
 C.   Fixed mortgage rate
 D.   Bridge loan

50. A tenant is legally allowed to remove equipment previously installed to facilitate business operations before the expiry of a lease. Why is this the case?

 A.   The equipment is considered trade fixtures
 B.   The equipment belongs to the lease holder
 C.   The lessor does not want it
 D.   It was part of the lease agreement

51. What type of easement attaches rights to an individual rather than the property?

 A.   Easement appurtenant
 B.   Easement in gross
 C.   Prescriptive easement
 D.   All of the above

52. What is the name given to the lowest section of the roof that extends into the sidewalls?

 A.   Board
 B.   Eaves
 C.   Joists
 D.   Beams

53. Which two parties are responsible for determining the commission earned by the broker?

 A.   Seller and agent
 B.   Seller and broker
 C.   Buyer and agent
 D.   Buyer and seller

54. Why must a lawsuit be filed within a specific time after an occurrence?

 A.   To prevent the criminal from getting away
 B.   Lis pendens
 C.   Credibility
 D.   Statute of limitations

55. Chris borrows money to purchase a new home and gives the mortgage to the lender as security. What term can be used to refer to Chris?

 A.   Mortgagor
 B.   Mortgagee
 C.   Broker
 D.   Buyer

56. What type of lease does a tenant have when he is paying a percentage of gross sales in addition to the base rent?

 A.   Proprietary lease
 B.   Net lease
 C.   Percentage lease
 D.   Gross lease

57. Why was the Civil Rights Act of 1866 significant in real estate?

   A. It protected against racial discrimination
   B. It protected interests of women
   C. It protected children's rights
   D. It protected against ageism

58. Why was the Privacy Act of 1974 significant?

   A. It required agencies to publicize records to the Federal Register
   B. It required privacy of records
   C. It required federal government to operate without transparency
   D. It required credit information to be kept private

59. Why was the Civil Liberties Act of 1988 significant?

   A. It granted all citizens equality
   B. It granted reparations to Japanese Americans interned by the government during World War II
   C. It passed rights to empower women in employment
   D. It passed rights to ensure fair housing

60. Jack is trying to convince Mary to sell her property in her neighborhood because it is changing due to the influx of people of other ethnic backgrounds. What is he doing?

   A. Steering
   B. Discriminating
   C. Blockbusting
   D. Convincing

61. What is the name of an agreement that allows for conditions on a property?

   A. Contract
   B. Deed
   C. Lease
   D. Qualified fee estate

62. What is **redlining**?

   A. Refusal by lending institutions to grant loans based on race
   B. Refusal by lending institutions to grant loans to people with poor credit scores
   C. Refusal of lending institutions to grant loans based on the agency being used for a purchase
   D. Refusal of a lending institution to make a loan because the area is integrated or populated by culturally diverse people

63. What is a form of co-ownership that involves a husband and wife having equal and undivided interest in the property?

   A. Joint tenancy
   B. Tenancy in common
   C. Tenancy by entirety
   D. Tenancy at will

64. What is the act of a property reverting to the state on death of the owner?

   A. Escheat
   B. Encumbrance
   C. Easement
   D. Suing

65. If you have a loan of $150,000 with an 8% interest, how much do you pay in interest every month?

   A. $1,000
   B. $1,200
   C. $5,000
   D. $12,000

66. Based on their contract, a lender declares the entire balance of the loan due immediately due to default by the borrower. How is this possible?

   A. Payday loans
   B. Alternative financing
   C. Acceleration clause
   D. Lines of credit

67. What type of payment plan allows a borrower to make smaller payments in the early years of a mortgage with payments increasing over time?

   A. Blanket mortgage
   B. Graduated mortgage
   C. Anomalous mortgage
   D. Balloon mortgage

68. What kind of mortgage should you apply for if you are buying more than an individual unit or plot?

   A. Graduated mortgage
   B. Blanket mortgage
   C. Balloon mortgage
   D. Adjustable rate mortgage

69. A salesperson is presented with two offers on a listed property. One is above the listing price and another below, which offer should he present to the seller?

   A. Both offers
   B. The one above the listing price
   C. The one below the listing price
   D. Neither

70. What is the name of a transaction where a seller finances the whole sale or part of the sale of a property for the buyer?

   A. Mortgage
   B. Refinancing
   C. Purchase money
   D. Buydown

71. What is an assessment of the value of a property as of a specific date based on objective data?

   A. CMA
   B. Listing price
   C. Tax value
   D. Appraisal

72. Which toxic metallic element is found in old paint and water pipes?

   A. Mercury
   B. Manganese
   C. Cadmium
   D. Lead

73. What is the amount of space used to calculate the lease payments which includes the shared property's common and service areas?

A. Rentable square footage
B. Usable square footage
C. Common areas
D. Service areas

74. Which chemical compounds commonly used in coolants and refrigeration contribute to the depletion of the ozone?

A. CFCs
B. Tetrafluoroethane
C. Anhydrous ammonia
D. Greenhouse gases

75. Which of the following does liability insurance protect you from?

A. House fire
B. Injury incurred on property
C. Flood
D. All of the above

76. What is a deed used for?

A. To transfer title rights
B. An official document proving a bank has loaned money
C. A pro forma statement
D. A lien

77. What is the measurement used to show the volatility of a market?

A. Absorption rate
B. Fluctuation rate
C. Inflation
D. Purchase deviation

78. What is the relationship between a broker and their client called?

A. Fiduciary
B. Trustee
C. Seller disclosure
D. Subagent

79. What is the law of agency?

A. Commissions that are collected from both parties
B. A set of laws that apply to a person who acts on behalf of another person
C. The ability to accept an offer on behalf of the seller
D. An authorized agency selling another's property

80. A severance is defined as _____.

A. Real property that is converted into personal property
B. Anything that is attached to the property naturally or by a person
C. A person that is acting under a power of attorney
D. An agreement between a lender and a borrower in which the borrower pledges collateral on a loan

81. _____ is the increase in value that occurs when combining two parcels into one large parcel.

   A.   Redlining
   B.   Plottage
   C.   Assemblage
   D.   Due diligence

82. What is a traffic report?

   A.   A. A list of property's a broker is selling at one time
   B.   A list of property that have been listed for sale in a specified area
   C.   The number of property's a licensed broker is managing
   D.   A list of prospects who have inquired or visited the property

83. What is the purpose of the Real Estate Settlement and Procedures Act?

   A.   Provide buyers and sellers with disclosures regarding settlement costs
   B.   Protect licensed brokers and agents from abusive practices regarding settlements
   C.   Ensure buyers and sellers have the ability to back out of settlements within 30 days
   D.   Pursue lawsuits against licensed brokers and agents on behalf of the client

84. _____ is also referred to as panic selling or panic peddling.

   A.   Redlining
   B.   Blockbusting
   C.   Amortization
   D.   Easement

85. A liability that consists of smaller payments of interest and principal and a balloon payment on the loan maturity date is a
_____.

    A. Term loan
    B. Fully amortized loan
    C. Partially amortized loan
    D. Balloon loan

86. When a real estate license is responsible for maintaining a client's property and maximizing the return on investment, the licensee is acting as a _____.

    A. Building manager
    B. Property manager
    C. Broker
    D. Rental agent

87. Which of the following is an example of agricultural real property?

    A. Farm
    B. Warehouse
    C. Condominium building
    D. All of the above

88. A _____ is a law that defines how property in specific geographic area can be used.

    A. National Association of Realtors
    B. Federal Reserve Board
    C. Zoning ordinance
    D. Fair Housing Act

89. What is the purpose of a real estate appraiser?

   A. Provide an estimate of a property's value based on selling price
   B. Provide a professional estimate of the property's market value
   C. Work with a borrower to provide the lender with an annual market value of a home
   D. All of the above

90. _____ measures the rental rates with the value of real property.

   A. Real estate broker
   B. Arbitration
   C. Gross rent multiplier
   D. Mortgagor

91. What is the approach that is used to appraise a home by comparing a property with other properties similar in size and condition in the same area?

   A. Sales approach
   B. Comparison appraisal
   C. Market comparison approach
   D. Market data approach

92. A _____ is a loan where the borrower pays a down payment of 20% and receives a loan of 80%.

   A. Non-conforming loan
   B. Conventional loan
   C. Real property agreement
   D. None of the above

93. A potential buyer has been denied a loan from a lender. The seller of the home allows the buyer to pay an agreed amount every month for ownership of the property. What is this type of agreement called?

    A. Contract for deed
    B. Rent to buy agreement
    C. Real property agreement
    D. None of the above

94. A real estate licensee makes a change to an original contract. They extend the closing date on a contract by 30 days. This change is called a(n) _____.

    A. Assumption
    B. Addendum
    C. Collusion
    D. Reconveyance

95. Which of the following is an example of adverse possession?

    A. A buyer forcibly buying a piece of property
    B. A tenant refusing to leave at the end of a lease
    C. Continuous use of a private road
    D. All of the above

96. Which clause protects an agent from a seller waiting for a listing agreement to end to avoid paying a commission to an agent?

    A. Survival clause
    B. Amendment
    C. Extension clause
    D. Protection clause

97. Which organization is the largest purchaser of home loans in the secondary market and serves to stimulate homeownership?

    A. Mortgage Bankers Association
    B. Federal National Mortgage Association (FNMA)
    C. Government National Mortgage Association
    D. The Mortgage Bank

98. What is the purpose of the U.S. Department of Housing and Urban Development (HUD)?

    A. To ensure everyone has access to fair and equal housing
    B. To provide low-income families with home loans
    C. To create government funded homes
    D. To regulate the housing market in the United States

99. Who oversee that Federal Housing Association?

    A. The Senate
    B. Federal National Mortgage Association
    C. U.S. Department of Housing and Urban Development
    D. States

100. The Equal Credit Opportunity Act (ECOA) prohibits lenders from discriminating against _____.

    A. Gender
    B. Marital status
    C. National origin
    D. All of the above

THIS IS THE END OF THE NATIONAL PORTION.

State Portion

1. Which statute governs the ad valorem taxation of property?

   A. Machinery Act
   B. General Statute
   C. The Ad Valorem Act
   D. Real Estate Taxation Act

2. Which type of valuation technique applies a standard percentage increase or decrease to all property in a specified location?

   A. Valuation
   B. County appraisal
   C. Mass appraisal
   D. There is no such appraisal

3. What is an octennial reappraisal?

   A. Grouping reappraisals by square footage and year built
   B. The statutory reappraisal of all real property in North Carolina for tax purposes
   C. Reappraisals done in groups of 8
   D. None of the above

4. The _____ is responsible for real estate licensing.

   A. Federal Real Estate Commission
   B. Housing and Urban Development
   C. North Carolina Real Estate Commission
   D. County clerk's office

5. Which type of lien provides security to persons that work on real property owned by others?

   A. Mortgage lien
   B. Mechanic's lien
   C. Real estate tax lien
   D. State income tax lien

6. Which of the following is a requirement to become a real estate broker in North Carolina?

   A. 18 years of age
   B. 90 hours of real estate courses
   C. Payment of an application fee
   D. All of the above

7. Which type of broker license status category is "entry level" and requires supervision?

   A. Provisional broker
   B. Broker in charge
   C. Broker
   D. There is no such license status category

8. Which statement is true about the North Carolina Real Estate Commission?

   A. They are a not-for-profit firm that manages real estate agents
   B. They are responsible for overseeing the licensing and regulating of real estate agents in North Carolina
   C. They are a private agency created to protect the real estate industry in the state of North Carolina
   D. None of the above

9. Which non-profit trade association represents 46 local real estate associations in North Carolina and provides opportunities and resources that aid the members?

   A. North Carolina Association of Realtors
   B. National Association of Real Estate Brokers
   C. The Association of Real Estate License Law Officials
   D. The National Association of Realtors

10. Which of the following statements is true about reciprocity in North Carolina?

   A. They must take the North Carolina licensing exam
   B. They must pay a fee for the nonresident license
   C. The licensee does not have to have an active license in the original state
   D. All of the above is true

11. Real estate applicants must provide proof that they possess _____,

   A. General moral character
   B. The ability to sell
   C. Organization skills
   D. Communication skills

12. Real estate applicants must provide proof that they possess _____,

   A. Broker in charge
   B. Provisional broker
   C. Managing broker
   D. Broker

13. Which of the following statements is true about brokers in the state of North Carolina?

   A. They have the ability to operate independently
   B. They must work under a broker in charge
   C. They have the ability to designate themselves as broker in charge
   D. A&C only

14. Which of the following statements is true about real estate education in North Carolina?

   A. Formal education is not required
   B. Courses must be at an approved real estate school
   C. Course can be for out of state exams as well
   D. All of the above is true

15. All personal property in the state of North Carolina is appraised at its true value. Which of the following is an exception to this?

   A. Inventories owned by manufacturers
   B. Inventories owned by wholesalers
   C. Rental property
   D. A&B only

16. Which of the following is a state North Carolina does not have reciprocity with?

   A. Arkansas
   B. West Virginia
   C. South Carolina
   D. Virginia

17. A real estate license in North Carolina is issued for a _____.

   A. 3-year period
   B. 5-year period
   C. 1-year period
   D. 10-year period

18. There is only one type of real estate license in North Carolina which is _____.

   A. Broker
   B. Provisional
   C. Sales agent
   D. Broker in charge

19. Which type of lien is given higher priority?

   A. Mortgage lien
   B. Current real estate taxes
   C. Mechanic's lien for work started prior to the mortgage
   D. None of the above

20. North Carolina requires all counties to conduct reappraisals at least every _____.

   A. 4 years
   B. 8 years
   C. 2 years
   D. 10 years

21. How many hours of continuing education must be completed during the renewal period?

    A. 25 hours
    B. 5 hours
    C. 10 hours
    D. 8 hours

22. Which of the following types of persons are exempt from real estate licensure?

    A. The property owner
    B. A family member of the property owner
    C. A broker from another state
    D. All of the above

23. The _____ are exempt from licensure in a partnership.

    A. W-2 salaried employees
    B. General partners
    C. Managers
    D. Directors

24. Which of the following job duties is a non-licensed employee of a real estate agency not allowed to do?

    A. Negotiate leases or rental agreements
    B. Provide a prospective tenant a rental price
    C. Complete and execute preprinted forms
    D. Accept security deposits and rental payments

25. Which of the following is true about unlicensed real estate assistants in North Carolina?

    A. They cannot be paid on commission

    B. They can be paid on a sales volume

    C. They cannot assist a license broker

    D. All of the above is true

26. In which of the following situations can a North Carolina broker file a lien to secure payment of brokerage fees?

    A. A listing agent for a $5 million property

    B. A person representing the lease of a manufacturing plant

    C. The sale of a shopping center by a listing agent

    D. The buyer's agent for a principal who is purchasing an office building

27. Ad valorem property tax rates can be adjusted every _____.

    A. Year

    B. 10 years

    C. 4 years

    D. 8 years

28. Which of the following duties can an unlicensed assistant in property management offices do?

    A. Show properties and rental units

    B. Accept applications

    C. Accept deposits and payments

    D. All of the above

29. Who chooses the members of the NCREC?

    A. General assembly
    B. Public voting
    C. Governor
    D. A&C only

30. How many members of the NCREC must be licensed brokers?

    A. 7
    B. 2
    C. 3
    D. 5

31. The members of the NCREC shall not do which of the following?

    A. Make rules or regulations regulating commission salaries
    B. Suspend or revoke a license at any time
    C. Take disciplinary action against a licensee who makes any willful or negligent misrepresentation of any material fact
    D. NCREC is allowed to do all of the above

32. North Carolina requires a broker to have a demand deposit in a _____.

    A. Commercial bank
    B. Federally insured depository institution
    C. Credit union
    D. Savings and loan association

33. The NCREC has the authority to issue a _____ for the appearance of witnesses deemed necessary to testify.

    A. Subpoena
    B. Lawsuit
    C. Request
    D. None of the above

34. An unlicensed person is practicing real estate in North Carolina, what action can the NCREC take?

    A. Fine the person
    B. Issue a cease-and-desist order
    C. Pursue disciplinary action
    D. None of the above

35. Who is responsible for setting guidelines for real estate education?

    A. Governor
    B. House of Representatives
    C. NCREC
    D. State Senators

36. A licensee may face disciplinary action if they do which of the following?

    A. Not meeting a sales quota
    B. Represents a real estate broker without their consent
    C. Fail to account for or remit monies coming into their possession
    D. B&C only

37. Who elects the NCREC chairman?

    A. The members of the NCREC
    B. Governor
    C. House of representatives
    D. A&B only

38. How many members of the NCREC are not allowed to be directly or indirectly involved in real estate or the real estate appraisal business?

    A. 7
    B. 2
    C. 1
    D. 5

39. How many members does the NCREC consist of?

    A. 5
    B. 10
    C. 9
    D. 8

40. Which of the following is not a requirement of the North Carolina mechanics liens?

    A. A vendor needs to file a mechanic's lien within 120 days of the delivery of the vendor's last labor or materials
    B. A lien agent is not required for a private construction project on a single-family home if the property is owner-occupied
    C. A vendor will forfeit the mechanic's lien priority if the vendor does not serve notice to the lien agent within 15 fays of furnishing material or labor
    D. A lien agent needs to be designated for private residential construction projects over $30,000 only

THIS IS THE END OF THE STATE PORTION.

Practice Test 1 – Answers

Answer Key – National Portion

1.	A	21.	A	41.	C	61.	D	81.	B
2.	B	22.	A	42.	B	62.	D	82.	D
3.	B	23.	B	43.	A	63.	C	83.	A
4.	A	24.	D	44.	D	64.	A	84.	B
5.	D	25.	C	45.	A	65.	A	85.	C
6.	B	26.	C	46.	C	66.	C	86.	B
7.	C	27.	C	47.	D	67.	B	87.	A
8.	D	28.	A	48.	B	68.	B	88.	C
9.	A	29.	D	49.	C	69.	A	89.	B
10.	B	30.	B	50.	A	70.	C	90.	C
11.	B	31.	D	51.	B	71.	D	91.	D
12.	A	32.	A	52.	B	72.	D	92.	B
13.	A	33.	A	53.	B	73.	A	93.	A
14.	C	34.	D	54.	D	74.	A	94.	B
15.	D	35.	A	55.	A	75.	D	95.	C
16.	A	36.	A	56.	C	76.	A	96.	D
17.	B	37.	D	57.	A	77.	A	97.	B
18.	C	38.	B	58.	A	78.	A	98.	A
19.	C	39.	B	59.	B	79.	B	99.	C
20.	D	40.	D	60.	C	80.	A	100.	D

1.   **A) A loan that has a predetermined repayment interest rate**

Commonly compared to floating rate, which is a loan that uses external factors as a benchmark for interest rates and is usually fluctuating based on the external market.

2.   **B) Civil Rights Act of 1866**

This act declares all citizens equal and under the protection of the law. The law emphasized protecting all citizens of African descent during the Civil War.

3.   **B) Promissory note**

This is a financial document by the issuer to the payee that contains a promise to make payment for a definite sum of money. It is usually valid for payment either on demand or on a specified date. It usually contains information regarding the principal amount, interest rate, date and place of issuance, maturity date and signature of the parties involved.

4.   **A) Refinancing**

This is the process of replacing an existing mortgage with another that offers more favorable terms to the borrower. Refinancing enables a borrower to negotiate for lower monthly payments, lower interest rates and renegotiate the loan payment term.

5.   **D) All of the above**

An appurtenance is real property fixed to the land that is passed along with the sale of a property.

6.   **B) Certificate of deposit**

This is a product offered by banks and credit facilities to customers enabling them to deposit a lump sum amount for a predetermined period with an agreed upon interest rate premium. Doing some research on the certificate of deposit terms offered by the different available facilities is important to yield better returns.

7.   **C) $250,000**

$225,000 / (1 - 0.1) = $250,000

8.   **D) Annual percentage rate**

This is the annual rate charged on a loan or investment. It is usually used to express the actual annual cost of funds over the lifespan of a loan or cash investment. As loan arrangements vary among institutions and the situation surrounding the loan, a standardized APR is set to protect borrowers from unreasonably high interest rates.

9.   **A) Public auctions**

Homes are usually put on auction due to default on a mortgage or property taxes. Buying a house at an auction is risky as it often does not give the buyer a chance to view the interior of the house. When buying a property at an auction, it is necessary to run background research on the property.

10.   **B) Pre-qualification**

These is the process of reviewing clients' creditworthiness and is usually used as a marketing strategy to obtain new clients. Creditors usually mail a potential borrower outlining maximum limit for loan.

11. **B) Power of attorney**

This is a legal document that transfers rights to act in place of a principal in the event that they are unable to act for themselves. The terms of the contract usually include what can be managed and where the power of the agent ends.

12. **A) Exclusive listing**

An exclusive listing is an agreement between a seller and an agent stating that commission on a sale can only be earned when a sale is made within a specified period of time. The timeframe for the sale is usually agreed on by both parties while entering the agreement.

13. **A) Single agency**

This is brokerage agreement where a buying agent is assigned the role to represent a buyer and works in single agency capacity as the buyer's agent. This agent is bound by fiduciary duties to the buyer and cannot disclose any confidential information to the other party.

14. **C) Arms-length transaction**

This is a transaction where both the buyer and the seller are acting in self-interest with an aim of getting the better deal. The discrepancy is usually solved when both parties agree on a middle ground that fulfills the interests of both the buyer and the seller.

15. **D) Adjustment date**

This is the changing of a date where calculations on items such as property taxes, rent and damage deposits are done.

16. **A) Assumable mortgage**

This is a mortgage arrangement that allows the seller to transfer the terms and conditions of a mortgage to a buyer. In this case, a buyer absorbs the seller's remaining debt instead of taking out a new mortgage.

17. **B) Call option**

This is a contract signed by both the buyer and the seller giving one party the right to sell and the other the right to buy a property on a future date. The price of the property is usually included in the contract and remains the same regardless of inflation or market shifts.

18. **C) A specified expiration date**

An exclusive listing contract is an agreement where a real estate agent receives commission within a specified amount of time. The agent receives commission no matter how the buyer is found.

19. **C) Reciprocity**

Real estate license reciprocity allows agents to obtain a real estate license in another state by taking the reciprocal state's exam.

20. **D) Privacy**

The 6 fiduciary duties of a real estate agent are: **O**bedience, **L**oyalty, **D**isclosure, **C**onfidentiality, **A**ccountability, and **R**easonable care / diligence (OLDCAR)

21. **A) Conditions that must be met by both the buyer and the seller before closing**

They are set in place to protect the parties involved in the contract. A breach in the contingencies results in the immediate termination of the contract.

22. **A) Any individual whose name appears on the loan document**

This is often someone whose credit score was taken into consideration when determining whether or not a loan can be extended. A co-borrower can be beneficial for a borrower that is unable to get favorable interest rates.

23. **B) Construction loan**

This is a short-term loan that is usually taken to finance the construction of a home or real estate property. It is usually taken to provide cash flow before larger funding is approved.

24. **D) Final walkthrough**

This is a visit done to the property by the buyer after all financing has been secured. A buyer is required to visit the premise and establish whether all the things that were discussed in the contract have been met prior to closing the deal.

25. **C) Fixed mortgage rate**

This is a mortgage loan whose interest rate remains the same throughout the longevity of the loan.

26. **C) Loan to value ratio**

This is defined as the percentage of the home's value owned by the borrower after making a down payment. It is calculated by taking the mortgage loan amount and dividing it by the appraisal value of the property being bought. The higher the loan to value ratio, the less likely lenders are to agree to loans.

27. **C) 20%**

($1,000 * 12) / $60,000 = 0.2

28. **A) Vicarious liability**

This is a secondary form of liability where a superior is held accountable for the actions of his subordinates. In the real estate sector, vicarious liability arises when an agent hired by either the buyer or seller acts inappropriately. In this case, the client is held accountable for the misconduct of his agent.

29. **D) Agency disclosure statement**

This is a statement signed by both the seller and buyer prior to the real estate transaction. Its role is to disclose the role of the agent in the transaction. An agent can either be a broker for either the buyer or the seller, a dual agent or a sub agent. In order to enforce disclosure laws, some states have a disclosure form written into law.

30. **B) Price fixing**

This is a situation that arises where a number of real estate agencies that dominate the market agree on a set commission. Brokers are required by law to set their individual commissions where consideration to the market going rate is allowed. Choosing to agree on a set standard commission could result in the suspension of a broker's license. These laws were set in place to protect the buyers and sellers in the market.

31. **D) IRS**

The IRS uses the general rule that an individual can be classified as an independent contractor if the payer has the right to control the result of work and not how it will be done.

32. **A) Freehold**

Freehold title is a title given to a freehold property where the owner owns the unit and the land on which the establishment has been developed and anything that is erected on the land.

33. **A) $0**

According to the Taxpayer Relief Act of 1997, a married couple is eligible for exemption from capital gain tax on profits of up to $500,000. This can only be claimed provided the property is the primary home of the selling couple meaning they have been living there for at least 2 years. Therefore, Mr. and Mrs. Smith do not owe anything in capital gain tax.

34. **D) Suspended**

He can choose to wait for the suspension to be lifted or look for another broker. A license can be suspended due to violation of insurance laws, providing materially misleading information and fraudulent practices. A revoked can only be reinstated after one year with undeniable evidence of trustworthiness and ability to uphold the law.

35. **A) Umbrella policy**

An umbrella insurance policy is an excess liability policy that is often used as a fail-safe for assets and savings. It is mostly used by people that are at risk of being sued. Contrary to popular belief, an umbrella policy does not cover additional risk area but acts as an addition to an already existing insurance.

36. **A) Comparative Market Analysis**

Comparative Market Analysis is never used in valuation as it is based on the market value of similar properties whereas no two real properties are alike.

37. **D) Voidable Contract**

A voidable contract is a formal agreement between parties that can be rendered obsolete due to legal factors. Some of the factors that can result in a voidable contract being rejected are fraud, undisclosed facts and a breach of the contract. A voidable contract is always considered legal unless rendered unenforceable.

38. **B) Disclosure**

Fiduciary duties arise when an agency operates on behalf of a client. In this case the agent is legally mandated to act in the best interest of the client. When an agent fails to disclose facts that may influence the final decision of the client, he is in violation of the disclosure clause.

39. **B) Joint tenancy**

A joint tenancy is an arrangement where two or more parties agree to co-own a property with equal rights and obligations. Upon death of a partner, the property remains solely in the ownership of the surviving partner. A joint tenancy has to be entered at the same time through a deed. Joint tenancy has the advantage of avoiding legal battles after the demise of a partner but can be hard to settle in the event of a divorced couple.

40. **D) Proprietary lease**

A proprietary lease is a is an agreement that allows a shareholder in a housing corporation to live in a unit equaling their stakes in the corporation. A shareholder does not buy the property but shares in the corporation. In this case, the shares act as collateral on the lease.

41. **C) Void**

This means to be obsolete and have no enforceable terms. Parties to a void contract are not bound by its terms making the contract unenforceable.

42. **B) 43,560**

An acre is a standard unit for measuring land. An acre does not have to be square shaped but contains an equivalent of 43560 square feet.

43. **A) 100 amps**

The minimum is 100 amps as anything below that may not be able to sustain the electric needs of a home. Larger homes can have between 150 and 200 amps based on the type of electronic systems installed. Having a proper electrical distribution in the home will also avoid trips.

44. **D) 75%**

750,000 / 1,000,000 = 0.75

The debt-to-equity ratio is used to determine whether a buyer can afford a house or to refinance an already owned property.

45. **A) FEMA**

The Federal Emergency Management Agency focuses on promoting the need to work together to support citizens and fast respondents. Its goal is to ensure citizens build and sustain to prepare for and recover from calamities.

46. **C) Blueprint**

A blueprint is a reproduction of a technical drawing on a light sensitive sheet that is done using a contact printer. A blueprint is usually required to predetermine the design and pattern that is going to be followed in a construction.

47. **D) UFFI**

Urea Formaldehyde Foam Insulation was used for house insulation in the 70s due to its high thermal resistance. Testing in the lab showed that the insulation produced fumes that were toxic for humans and the environment leading to its ban in 1982.

48. **B) Dual agency**

Dual agency is legal in Pennsylvania provided both the buyer and the seller agree to the arrangement after pros and cons of the relationship are laid on the table. Opting to have a dual agent means that the client cannot expect the agent to act in their best interest as he is representing two conflicting interests.

49. **C) Fixed mortgage rate**

This is an agreement between the seller and agent conveying that the agent is eligible for commission on the sale of the property regardless of who found the buyer. The terms of the agreement are only valid for a sale made within the time period of the agreement.

50. **A) The equipment is considered trade fixtures**

Trade fixtures are removable personal property that are installed in a leased space to facilitate business running. For one to be allowed to remove a fixture, it must be essential for the running of the business to not cause damage to the property and be removed before the expiry of the lease.

51. **B) Easement in gross**

The rights associated by the easement are irrevocable for the person granted. A transfer of the property to another individual through sale or inheritance does not warrant an automatic transfer of the rights to the new owner. This renders the easement of gross void.

52. **B) Eaves**

An eave is the lower edge of a roof that protrude or hangs over the building's side.

53. **B) Seller and broker**

The seller and broker are usually responsible for agreeing in the amount of commission that should be paid to the broker

54. **D) Statute of limitations**

The statute of limitations is a law that sets the maximum period of time parties involved in a rift have to initiate legal proceedings from the day of the occurrence of the event. The time allocated to offences differs according to the nature of the offence.

55. **A) Mortgagor**

A mortgagor is an individual that borrows money from a lender in order to purchase a property. The lending is based on the individual's credit score and collateral. A title must be handed to the lender as collateral for the loan.

56. **C) Percentage lease**

A percentage lease is a type of lease where the tenant pays rent plus a percentage of any revenue earned while doing business on the property. This agreement significantly reduces the rent paid. The parties involved agree on a base point where percentage lease kicks in.

57. **A) It protected against racial discrimination**

The Civil Rights act of 1866 banned racial discrimination in real estate and housing transactions. People of any race had equal rights as whites to buy, sell, or lease property.

58. **A) It required agencies to publicize records to the Federal Register**

The Privacy Act of 1974 is an act that established code of fair information maintenance governing the collection, use and maintenance of individuals that is maintained by federal agencies. The act required the agencies to publicize the records in the Federal Register.

59. **B) It granted reparations to Japanese Americans interned by the government during World War II**

The Civil Liberties Act of 1988 granted the Japanese Americans that has been interned by the government during World War 2 reparation.

60. **C) Blockbusting**

This is the act of trying to manipulate tenants to sell or rent their properties at lower rates due to an influx of minority groups in a once segregated neighborhood.

61. **D) Qualified fee estate**

This is an estate agreement that facilitates the grantor to propose a set of conditions. A breach in the condition limitation may result in termination of the agreement. A quality fee estate can also be based on the occurrence of a predetermined event.

62. **D) Refusal of a lending institution to make a loan because the area is integrated or populated by culturally diverse people**

This usually occurs when a lending institution has a map of areas they would not like to initiate credit in. Potential property owners are denied mortgages despite great credit scores due to the location of the property they intend to purchase.

63. **C) Tenancy by entirety**

Only married couples can enter this type of co-ownership where the property is jointly owned as a single entity. It facilitates right of survivorship and can be terminated upon death of spouse or divorce.

64. **A) Escheat**

A property can be reverted to the state if no claimants have come forth to claim the property or the available heir has been deemed legally unfit to be granted ownership. It is revocable once a legal heir claims the property.

65. **A) $1,000**

($150,000 * 0.08) / 12 = $1,000

66. **C) Acceleration clause**

This is a contract that allows a lender to require full settlement of an outstanding loan due to a breach of predetermined conditions.

67. **B) Graduated mortgage**

This is a fixed price loan that allows the borrower to make smaller payments on the loan in the earlier payment years and continues to increase gradually until the mortgage is paid off. It considers individuals who were otherwise not qualified for the higher rate to qualify.

68. **B) Blanket mortgage**

A blanket mortgage is a mortgage that covers two or more pieces of real estate. The real estate property is held as collateral. Individual properties can be sold without having to retire the mortgage. This insurance is usually taken when purchasing and developing land.

69. **A) Both offers**

The agent is required by fiduciary duties to present both the offers to the client. Choosing to present the higher offer to the client in order to reap higher commission from the sale is a breach of fiduciary duties.

70. **C) Purchase money**

This is a mortgage issued by the seller as part of a real estate transaction. This arrangement is usually reached when the buyer is not eligible for the traditional mortgage. A down payment is usually placed on the property as an order of the financial transaction.

71. **D) Appraisal**

An appraisal is an opinion usually given by a professional on the market value of a property. Properties usually require an appraisal is unique and market value of similar properties may not offer an accurate value of the property.

72. **D) Lead**

Lead is a periodic metal that was used in paint in the 1970s as it accelerated drying, maintained a fresh appearance and resisted moisture. Older plumbing systems used lead lines and water often corroded the material as it was transported to the consumer's taps. Use of lead in paint was discontinued as it was found to cause nervous system damage and stunted growth in children.

73.   **A) Rentable square footage**

Rentable square footage is inclusive of the usable square footage and common areas. The price per rentable square foot is usually calculated using a pro-rata calculation based on the size of the space being leased.

74.   **A) CFCs**

CFCs are nonflammable chemicals that are commonly used in aerosol sprays and industrial cleaning products. Once these chemicals are released into the atmosphere they rise into the stratosphere where ultraviolet rays from the sun break them down. This breakdown releases chlorine atoms that destroy ozone molecules therefore forming ozone holes.

75.   **D) All of the above**

Liability insurance covers everything from house fires, injuries incurred on the property, floods, injured domestic workers, falling trees, and more.

76.   **A) To transfer title rights**

The buyer and seller must both sign a deed to transfer the property's ownership.

77.   **A) Absorption rate**

This is a ration of the number of properties that have been sold against the number of properties that are available for sale within a specified area.

78.   **A) Fiduciary**

Fiduciary is the relationship between client and broker. An agent is the fiduciary of the client.

79.   **B) A set of laws that apply to a person who acts on behalf of another person**

The law of agency is a set of duties that real estate professionals owe to their clients, including disclosures that must be made to the client. These duties are set by each state.

80.   **A) Real property that is converted into personal property**

There are two types of severance, actual severance and constructive severance. An actual severance is when an item is removed from the land and a constructive severance is when an item is detached by intent.

81.   **B) Plottage**

Plottage occurs when the total value of a combined parcel is worth more than the sum of the individual parcels. The process of combining the parcel is called assemblage.

82. **D) A list of prospects who have inquired or visited the property**

A traffic report keeps a count of prospective buyers who have called about or visited the property.

83. **A) Provide buyers and sellers with disclosures regarding settlement costs**

RESPA is a consumer protection act that provides procedures that need to be followed in one-to-four residential real estate sales. It assists in eliminating abusive practices during settlements, bars kickback and limits the use of escrow accounts

84. **B) Blockbusting**

An illegal act that is not permitted by the Fair Housing Laws. This method manipulates homeowners into selling or renting their home at a lower price by falsely stating that minorities (racial, religious, etc.,) are moving into a once segregated neighborhood.

85. **C) Partially amortized loan**

A partially amortized loan is a loan that involves partial amortization during the loan term and a lump sum on the loan maturity date.

86. **B) Property manager**

A property manager is responsible for maintaining a client's property and maximizing the return on the client's investment. When a licensee acts on behalf of a client and doing the above, they are acting as a property manager.

87. **A) Farm**

A farm is an example of an agricultural real property. Agricultural real property is property that is used for farming and can be the farmers real presence.

88. **C) Zoning ordinance**

A zoning ordinance specifies which zones can be used for residential or commercial purposes. It may also regulate the lot size, placement, bulk and height of the structures.

89. **B) Provides a professional estimate of the property's market value**

A real estate appraiser is responsible for providing an estimate of a property's market value. This is established by using appraisal methods and a trained, professional judgement.

90. **C) Gross rent multiplier**

The gross rent multiplier is the ratio of the price of an investment property to its annual rental income. This ratio is prior to accounting for expenses like insurance, utilities, and property taxes.

91. **D) Market data approach**

The market data approach, also called sales comparison approach, finds value of property by comparing it to other properties that are similar in size and condition. The properties are also in the same area. Appraisers will typically use comparable homes that were sold within 6 months of the appraisal.

92. **B) Conventional loan**

In a conventional loan a borrower pays a down payment of 20% and receives a loan for the remaining 80%. There is not government involvement in a conventional loan.

93. **A) Contract for deed**

A contract for deed or an installment contract is a simpler way for a buyer to buy a home. It is an agreement between the seller and the buyer that the buyer will pay a monthly payment to the seller and the deed to the home is turned over to the buyer when all payments have been made.

94. **B) Addendum**

An addendum is a change made to an original contract. The addendum is also called an amendment.

95. **C) Continuous use of a private road**

Adverse possession allows a person to claim a property right owned by another person. The person can gain the title by using another's property continuously, openly and without permission for a certain period of time. It is also called squatter's rights.

96. **D) Protection clause**

This clause entitles a real estate broker to a commission after the listing is expired or canceled. It is only valid if buyers have viewed the property.

97. **B) Federal National Mortgage Association (FNMA)**

The FNMA is a government sponsored enterprise that serves to stimulate homeownership. It is the largest purchaser of home loans and raises money to buy notes from lenders.

98. **A) To ensure everyone has access to fair and equal housing**

   HUD is tasked with providing housing and community development assistance, and ensure everyone has access to fair and equal housing. The mission is to create strong, sustainable and inclusive communities and provide quality and affordable homes to everyone.

99. **C) U.S. Department of Housing and Urban Development**

   The FHA provides mortgage insurance on loans that are made by FHA approved lenders. They insure single family homes, multi-family properties, hospitals and residential care facilities.

100. **D) All of the above**

   The ECOA prohibits discrimination in lending due to race, color, sex, religion, marital status, national origin and age.

Answer Key – State Portion

1.	A	21.	D
2.	C	22.	A
3.	B	23.	B
4.	C	24.	A
5.	B	25.	A
6.	D	26.	C
7.	A	27.	A
8.	B	28.	D
9.	A	29.	D
10.	B	30.	C
11.	A	31.	A
12.	A	32.	B
13.	D	33.	A
14.	B	34.	B
15.	D	35.	C
16.	D	36.	D
17.	C	37.	A
18.	A	38.	B
19.	B	39.	C
20.	B	40.	D

1.   **A) Machinery Act**

This act provides a framework for listing, appraising, and assessing real and personal property.

2.   **C) Mass Appraisal**

This is a valuation technique that is sometimes used for tax assessment purposes. It is also referred to as a horizontal adjustment.

3.   **B) The statutory reappraisal of all real property in North Carolina for tax purposes**

This is an octennial reappraisal and requires all counties to reappraise property within in a specified time period.

4.   **C) North Carolina Real Estate Commission**

This commission is responsible for real estate licensees, education, and other resources regarding real estate in the state of North Carolina.

5. **B) Mechanic's lien**

This type of lien is typically used to guarantee of payment to builders, contractors, and construction firms.

6. **D) All of the above**

All of the above are requirements to become a real estate agent in North Carolina. The real estate courses must be approved and in a classroom setting.

7. **A) Provisional broker**

This is an entry level license status and only requires 75 hours of pre-licensing education and passing of the license examination.

8. **B) They are responsible for overseeing the licensing and regulating of real estate agents in North Carolina**

This is an independent state governmental agency that oversees over 80,000 agents. They managing licensing requirements, laws, exams, renewal information, forms and more.

9. **A) North Carolina Association of Realtors**

This state organization is non-profit and was founded in 1921. It is one of the largest and most influential state associations in the state. It has a membership of over 47,000 professionals.

10. **B) They must pay a fee for the nonresident license**

Other rules for reciprocity include the agent must be in good standing and have an active license in the original state and a salesperson license must be actively and personally supervised by a licensee in North Carolina.

11. **A) General moral character**

The applicant must possess general moral character as well as competency, honesty, truthfulness, and integrity.

12. **A) Broker in charge**

A broker in charge has supervision over provisional brokers who are engaged in real estate at a specified office.

13. **D) A&C only**

A broker has the opportunity to operate independently as a sole proprietor or work for an agency. They have the ability to designate themselves as broker in charge if they qualify.

14. **B) Courses must be at an approved real estate school**

This is true for both continuing education and for prelicensure. Continuing education for renewal must be completed by June 10th of each year.

15. **D) A&B only**

Inventories owned by manufacturers, wholesalers, retailers and contracts, and non-business personal property are exempt.

16. **D) Virginia**

Virginia is a state that does not have reciprocity with North Carolina. Other states North Carolina has reciprocity with is Connecticut, Georgia, Iowa, Louisiana, Mississippi, Nebraska, and Tennessee.

17. **C) 1-year period**

The North Carolina license expires every year on June 30th and the license can be renewed 45 days prior to the expiration.

18. **A) Broker**

While there is only one type of real estate license in North Carolina, there are numerous types of license status categories such as provision broker and broker in charge.

19. **B) Current real estate taxes**

Liens regarding real estate take precedence over other types of liens. This type of lien gives creditors a way to collect debts owed to them.

20. **B) 8 years**

The machinery act states that all counties must conduct a reappraisal every 8 years. A majority of counties conduct reappraisals within 8 years and some conduct reappraisals every 4 years.

21. **D) 8 hours**

There are 8 hours of continuing education that must be completed to renew the license on active status. The courses must be completed by June 10th.

22.   **A) The property owner**

The owner of a property has the right to sell his or her property without a real estate license.

23.   **B) General partners**

In a partnership, the general partners are exempt from licensure, for an LLC it is the managers and for a corporation it is the directors, officers, and W-2 salaried employees.

24.   **A) Negotiate leases or rental agreements**

The unlicensed employee can do all of the above except negotiate leases or rental agreements. They also may not cold call or prospect for clients or show properties or open houses.

25.   **A) They cannot be paid on commission**

The unlicensed assistant cannot be paid on commission nor on a sales basis. They must also be paid on a salary or an hourly basis.

26.   **C) The sale of a shopping center by a listing agent**

The listing agent who has listed a shipping center, is about to file a lien to secure unpaid payments of brokerage fees.

27.   **A) Year**

The ad valorem property tax can be assessed every year. Ad valorem property tax is based on the value of property. North Carolina is an ad valorem property tax rate.

28.   **D) All of the above**

Assistants in property management offices without a license can do all of the above. They are able to accept payments and deposits, applications, and show properties and rental units.

29.   **D) A&C only**

7 of the members are appointed by the governor and 2 by general assembly. 1 of the members appointed by the general assembly is appointed on the recommendation of the President Pro Tempore and the other on the recommendation of the Speaker of the House of Representatives.

30.   **C) 3**

3 members of the NCREC need to be licensed brokers, the rest of the members do not need to be licensed brokers.

31.   **A) Make rules or regulations regulating commission salaries**

The NCREC cannot make rules or regulations regulating salaries or fees to be charged by licensees. They can, however revoke or suspend licenses and take disciplinary actions against a licensee.

32.   **B) Federally insured depository institution**

The account must be in a federally insured depository institution, which is a bank or savings association that insures the deposit by the federal deposit insurance corporation.

33.   **A) Subpoena**

The NREC has the authority to issue a subpoena for the appearance of witnesses deemed necessary to testify before or investigated by the commission. They may also issue a subpoena for records, documents, or other materials necessary for the investigation.

34.   **B) Issue a cease-and-desist order**

While the NREC does not have the authority to discipline a non-licensed person, they do have the power to issue a cease-and-desist order.

35.   **C) NCREC**

The NCREC is responsible for creating educational guidelines for real estate. They also are responsible for creating rules and regulations that are consistent with statutes.

36.   **D) B&C only**

Other reasons a licensee can face disciplinary action is accepting commission from anyone other than BIC or a broker, make false promises of character to influence, persuade or induce, and make willful or negligent misrepresentation or omission of any material fact.

37.   **A) The members of the NCREC**

The members of NCREC elect a chairman each year. There are 9 members of the NCREC all of whom serve 3-year terms.

38. **B) 2**

    2 members of the NCREC cannot be involved directly or indirectly in the real estate or real estate appraisal business. The rest are allowed to be directly and indirectly involved in real estate or real estate appraisal business.

39. **C) 9**

    The commission consists of 9 members and they serve 3 terms each. The terms are staggered.

40. **D) A lien agent needs to be designated for private residential construction projects over $30,000 only**

    The above is not a requirement of the North Carolina mechanic's lien. The other options are, the notice must be served within 15 days of the first furnishing materials, a lien is not required if the property is owner-occupied, and the mechanic's lien must be filed within 120 days of delivery of the last labor or materials.

Practice Test 2

Directions:

1. You have a 4-hour time limit to complete the whole exam.

2. To pass, you must answer at least 71 out of 100 questions correctly on the national portion **AND** at least 29 out of 40 questions on the state portion.

3. Some questions will require mathematics. You may use a calculator.

4. **Phones and pagers are not allowed. Having either will result in automatic dismissal from the exam and nullification of exam scores.**

Tips:

- Answer all questions even if you are unsure.
- Mark any questions you are stuck on and revisit them after you are done. The exam is timed so make sure you finish as many questions as you can.
- After reading the question, try answering it in your head first to avoid getting confused by the choices.
- Read the entire question before looking at the answers.
- Use the process of elimination to filter out choices that don't seem correct to increase your chances of selecting the correct answer.
- Be aware of important keywords like **not, sometimes, always,** and **never**. These words completely alter the ask of the question so it's important to keep track of them.

PLEASE READ THESE INSTRUCTIONS CAREFULLY.

Name: _____   Date: _____

NATIONAL PORTION

1.	Ⓐ Ⓑ Ⓒ Ⓓ	31.	Ⓐ Ⓑ Ⓒ Ⓓ	61.	Ⓐ Ⓑ Ⓒ Ⓓ	91.	Ⓐ Ⓑ Ⓒ Ⓓ
2.	Ⓐ Ⓑ Ⓒ Ⓓ	32.	Ⓐ Ⓑ Ⓒ Ⓓ	62.	Ⓐ Ⓑ Ⓒ Ⓓ	92.	Ⓐ Ⓑ Ⓒ Ⓓ
3.	Ⓐ Ⓑ Ⓒ Ⓓ	33.	Ⓐ Ⓑ Ⓒ Ⓓ	63.	Ⓐ Ⓑ Ⓒ Ⓓ	93.	Ⓐ Ⓑ Ⓒ Ⓓ
4.	Ⓐ Ⓑ Ⓒ Ⓓ	34.	Ⓐ Ⓑ Ⓒ Ⓓ	64.	Ⓐ Ⓑ Ⓒ Ⓓ	94.	Ⓐ Ⓑ Ⓒ Ⓓ
5.	Ⓐ Ⓑ Ⓒ Ⓓ	35.	Ⓐ Ⓑ Ⓒ Ⓓ	65.	Ⓐ Ⓑ Ⓒ Ⓓ	95.	Ⓐ Ⓑ Ⓒ Ⓓ
6.	Ⓐ Ⓑ Ⓒ Ⓓ	36.	Ⓐ Ⓑ Ⓒ Ⓓ	66.	Ⓐ Ⓑ Ⓒ Ⓓ	96.	Ⓐ Ⓑ Ⓒ Ⓓ
7.	Ⓐ Ⓑ Ⓒ Ⓓ	37.	Ⓐ Ⓑ Ⓒ Ⓓ	67.	Ⓐ Ⓑ Ⓒ Ⓓ	97.	Ⓐ Ⓑ Ⓒ Ⓓ
8.	Ⓐ Ⓑ Ⓒ Ⓓ	38.	Ⓐ Ⓑ Ⓒ Ⓓ	68.	Ⓐ Ⓑ Ⓒ Ⓓ	98.	Ⓐ Ⓑ Ⓒ Ⓓ
9.	Ⓐ Ⓑ Ⓒ Ⓓ	39.	Ⓐ Ⓑ Ⓒ Ⓓ	69.	Ⓐ Ⓑ Ⓒ Ⓓ	99.	Ⓐ Ⓑ Ⓒ Ⓓ
10.	Ⓐ Ⓑ Ⓒ Ⓓ	40.	Ⓐ Ⓑ Ⓒ Ⓓ	70.	Ⓐ Ⓑ Ⓒ Ⓓ	100.	Ⓐ Ⓑ Ⓒ Ⓓ
11.	Ⓐ Ⓑ Ⓒ Ⓓ	41.	Ⓐ Ⓑ Ⓒ Ⓓ	71.	Ⓐ Ⓑ Ⓒ Ⓓ		
12.	Ⓐ Ⓑ Ⓒ Ⓓ	42.	Ⓐ Ⓑ Ⓒ Ⓓ	72.	Ⓐ Ⓑ Ⓒ Ⓓ		
13.	Ⓐ Ⓑ Ⓒ Ⓓ	43.	Ⓐ Ⓑ Ⓒ Ⓓ	73.	Ⓐ Ⓑ Ⓒ Ⓓ		
14.	Ⓐ Ⓑ Ⓒ Ⓓ	44.	Ⓐ Ⓑ Ⓒ Ⓓ	74.	Ⓐ Ⓑ Ⓒ Ⓓ		
15.	Ⓐ Ⓑ Ⓒ Ⓓ	45.	Ⓐ Ⓑ Ⓒ Ⓓ	75.	Ⓐ Ⓑ Ⓒ Ⓓ		
16.	Ⓐ Ⓑ Ⓒ Ⓓ	46.	Ⓐ Ⓑ Ⓒ Ⓓ	76.	Ⓐ Ⓑ Ⓒ Ⓓ		
17	Ⓐ Ⓑ Ⓒ Ⓓ	47.	Ⓐ Ⓑ Ⓒ Ⓓ	77.	Ⓐ Ⓑ Ⓒ Ⓓ		
18.	Ⓐ Ⓑ Ⓒ Ⓓ	48.	Ⓐ Ⓑ Ⓒ Ⓓ	78.	Ⓐ Ⓑ Ⓒ Ⓓ		
19.	Ⓐ Ⓑ Ⓒ Ⓓ	49.	Ⓐ Ⓑ Ⓒ Ⓓ	79.	Ⓐ Ⓑ Ⓒ Ⓓ		
20.	Ⓐ Ⓑ Ⓒ Ⓓ	50.	Ⓐ Ⓑ Ⓒ Ⓓ	80.	Ⓐ Ⓑ Ⓒ Ⓓ		
21.	Ⓐ Ⓑ Ⓒ Ⓓ	51.	Ⓐ Ⓑ Ⓒ Ⓓ	81.	Ⓐ Ⓑ Ⓒ Ⓓ		
22.	Ⓐ Ⓑ Ⓒ Ⓓ	52.	Ⓐ Ⓑ Ⓒ Ⓓ	82.	Ⓐ Ⓑ Ⓒ Ⓓ		
23.	Ⓐ Ⓑ Ⓒ Ⓓ	53.	Ⓐ Ⓑ Ⓒ Ⓓ	83.	Ⓐ Ⓑ Ⓒ Ⓓ		
24.	Ⓐ Ⓑ Ⓒ Ⓓ	54.	Ⓐ Ⓑ Ⓒ Ⓓ	84.	Ⓐ Ⓑ Ⓒ Ⓓ		
25.	Ⓐ Ⓑ Ⓒ Ⓓ	55.	Ⓐ Ⓑ Ⓒ Ⓓ	85.	Ⓐ Ⓑ Ⓒ Ⓓ		
26.	Ⓐ Ⓑ Ⓒ Ⓓ	56.	Ⓐ Ⓑ Ⓒ Ⓓ	86.	Ⓐ Ⓑ Ⓒ Ⓓ		
27.	Ⓐ Ⓑ Ⓒ Ⓓ	57.	Ⓐ Ⓑ Ⓒ Ⓓ	87.	Ⓐ Ⓑ Ⓒ Ⓓ		
28.	Ⓐ Ⓑ Ⓒ Ⓓ	58.	Ⓐ Ⓑ Ⓒ Ⓓ	88.	Ⓐ Ⓑ Ⓒ Ⓓ		
29.	Ⓐ Ⓑ Ⓒ Ⓓ	59.	Ⓐ Ⓑ Ⓒ Ⓓ	89.	Ⓐ Ⓑ Ⓒ Ⓓ		
30.	Ⓐ Ⓑ Ⓒ Ⓓ	60.	Ⓐ Ⓑ Ⓒ Ⓓ	90.	Ⓐ Ⓑ Ⓒ Ⓓ		

Name: _____   Date: _____

STATE PORTION

1.	Ⓐ Ⓑ Ⓒ Ⓓ	31.	Ⓐ Ⓑ Ⓒ Ⓓ
2.	Ⓐ Ⓑ Ⓒ Ⓓ	32.	Ⓐ Ⓑ Ⓒ Ⓓ
3.	Ⓐ Ⓑ Ⓒ Ⓓ	33.	Ⓐ Ⓑ Ⓒ Ⓓ
4.	Ⓐ Ⓑ Ⓒ Ⓓ	34.	Ⓐ Ⓑ Ⓒ Ⓓ
5.	Ⓐ Ⓑ Ⓒ Ⓓ	35.	Ⓐ Ⓑ Ⓒ Ⓓ
6.	Ⓐ Ⓑ Ⓒ Ⓓ	36.	Ⓐ Ⓑ Ⓒ Ⓓ
7.	Ⓐ Ⓑ Ⓒ Ⓓ	37.	Ⓐ Ⓑ Ⓒ Ⓓ
8.	Ⓐ Ⓑ Ⓒ Ⓓ	38.	Ⓐ Ⓑ Ⓒ Ⓓ
9.	Ⓐ Ⓑ Ⓒ Ⓓ	39.	Ⓐ Ⓑ Ⓒ Ⓓ
10.	Ⓐ Ⓑ Ⓒ Ⓓ	40.	Ⓐ Ⓑ Ⓒ Ⓓ
11.	Ⓐ Ⓑ Ⓒ Ⓓ		
12.	Ⓐ Ⓑ Ⓒ Ⓓ		
13.	Ⓐ Ⓑ Ⓒ Ⓓ		
14.	Ⓐ Ⓑ Ⓒ Ⓓ		
15.	Ⓐ Ⓑ Ⓒ Ⓓ		
16.	Ⓐ Ⓑ Ⓒ Ⓓ		
17	Ⓐ Ⓑ Ⓒ Ⓓ		
18.	Ⓐ Ⓑ Ⓒ Ⓓ		
19.	Ⓐ Ⓑ Ⓒ Ⓓ		
20.	Ⓐ Ⓑ Ⓒ Ⓓ		
21.	Ⓐ Ⓑ Ⓒ Ⓓ		
22.	Ⓐ Ⓑ Ⓒ Ⓓ		
23.	Ⓐ Ⓑ Ⓒ Ⓓ		
24.	Ⓐ Ⓑ Ⓒ Ⓓ		
25.	Ⓐ Ⓑ Ⓒ Ⓓ		
26.	Ⓐ Ⓑ Ⓒ Ⓓ		
27.	Ⓐ Ⓑ Ⓒ Ⓓ		
28.	Ⓐ Ⓑ Ⓒ Ⓓ		
29.	Ⓐ Ⓑ Ⓒ Ⓓ		
30.	Ⓐ Ⓑ Ⓒ Ⓓ		

National Portion

1. What is the process of attempting to recover a loan from a borrower that has stopped making payments?

   A. Concession
   B. Final walk through
   C. Foreclosure
   D. Private mortgage insurance

2. What fibrous material causes cancer when released into the air?

   A. Asbestos
   B. Cotton
   C. Textiles
   D. Trunks

3. What are the vertical beams that frame the house?

   A. Frames
   B. Joists
   C. Shingles
   D. Studs

4. What is a reason a broker may be suspended or have their license revoked?

   A. Misrepresentation
   B. Failure to retain clients
   C. Failure to sell property within specified timeframe
   D. None of the above

5. A property manager makes routine rounds to repair air conditioning vents. What is the term used to refer to this?

   A. Aesthetic maintenance
   B. Avoiding depreciation
   C. Preventive maintenance
   D. Proration

6. What is another term that can be used to refer to the lender?

   A. Seller
   B. Mortgagee
   C. Mortgagor
   D. Loanee

7. If a seller nets $150,000 from the sale of her home, and the commission is 4%, how much did the home sell for?

   A. $144,000
   B. $148,500
   C. $156,000
   D. $156,250

8. What is the name given to the restriction of land usage by the local authorities?

   A. Building codes
   B. Denial
   C. Land zoning
   D. Property tax

9. What is the lender required to do once it is a borrower is unable to clear a mortgage?

   A. Threaten borrower
   B. Sell property without court order
   C. Initiate judicial foreclosure
   D. Evict the borrower

10. Which association represents title insurance?

   A. American Land Title Association
   B. CERCLA
   C. Fair Housing Act
   D. FEMA

11. Which law was passed to regulate credit bureaus?

   A. Annuity law
   B. Consumer credit law
   C. Fair Credit Reporting Act
   D. Truth in Lending Act

12. What is the legal right granted to exit a property?

   A. Easement
   B. Escheat
   C. Right of egress
   D. Right of ingress

13. What is the name given to non-monetary investment?

   A. Sweat equity
   B. Investment
   C. Capital
   D. Maintenance

14. What type of arrangement allows a borrower to negotiate a lower interest rate?

   A. Buydown
   B. Mortgage
   C. Purchase money
   D. Purchase price

15. What is a title without any lien?

   A. Clear title
   B. Deed
   C. Freehold
   D. Regular title

16. What is the name given to the breakdown of an individual's credit history?

   A. Credit assessment
   B. Credit report
   C. Financial record
   D. Repayment report

17. What is another term used to describe ownership?

    A. Credit
    B. Equity
    C. Liability
    D. Shares

18. What is the notice filed against a borrower on missing the repayment deadline?

    A. Notice of cessation
    B. Notice to cure
    C. Notice of default
    D. Notice of intention

19. What is the name given to describe the period a lender must keep a loan offer open to the borrower?

    A. Due diligence period
    B. Loan repayment period
    C. Lock-in period
    D. Target hold period

20. Which of the following is a lease break?

    A. When a tenant breaks a rent prior to the date of expiry without a legal reason
    B. When a tenant terminates a contract once the lease has expired
    C. When a tenant breaks a lease with the agreement of the landlord
    D. When a landlord allows a tenant to sublease his residence

21. What is the term used to refer to a situation where the amount of funds required to meet an obligation are **not** available?

    A. Buydown
    B. Debt to income ratio
    C. Escrow
    D. Shortfall

22. What is the term used to describe a situation where taxes are reduced or completely scrapped to increase buyers in the market?

    A. Tax abatement
    B. Tax exemption
    C. Tax evasion
    D. Duty free

23. A property originally assessed at $500,000 appreciated at 4% the first year and then 5% the year after. What is its current value?

    A. $525,000
    B. $545,000
    C. $546,000
    D. None of the above

24. Which entity performs the percolation test?

    A. Department of State
    B. Building Inspector
    C. Homeowners Association
    D. Department of Health

25. If a property is taxed at 25% with a tax levy of $92,000, what is its assessed value?

    A. $65,000
    B. $115,000
    C. $122,666
    D. $368,000

26. What is the name given to a brief summary of the history of a title?

    A. Abstract of title
    B. Chain of title
    C. Deed chain
    D. History of deed

27. What material is used in construction to cover joints where two or more types of materials meet?

    A. Flashing
    B. Metal
    C. Wood
    D. Joint

28. What is the lowest section of the roof that overhangs beyond the sidewalls of the building?

    A. Eaves
    B. Joists
    C. Stud
    D. Shingles

29. Which real estate metric is found by dividing cash flow by the deposit and settlement costs?

    A. Cash out
    B. Cash on cash return
    C. Lock in period
    D. Loan to value ratio

30. Which board committee is responsible for maintaining the aesthetic view of a town?

    A. Architectural Review Board
    B. Federal government
    C. Municipality
    D. HOA

31. What type of lease is taken on a loft?

    A. Net lease
    B. Gross lease
    C. Percentage lease
    D. Proprietary lease

32. What clause can prohibit having loud parties?

    A. House rules
    B. Regulations
    C. Lease terms
    D. Noise permit

33. What is the measurement used to show the volatility of a market?

    A.   Fluctuation rate
    B.   Absorption rate
    C.   Inflation
    D.   Purchase deviation

34. What is the mortgage clause that allows a lender the right to demand immediate payment of a mortgage?

    A.   Cancellation clause
    B.   Acceleration clause
    C.   Prepayment Penalty clause
    D.   Release clause

35. Which agreement allows a property holder to cross another person's land?

    A.   Easement appurtenant
    B.   Easement in gross
    C.   Prescriptive easement
    D.   None of the above

36. Which of the following is insurance taken out as a protection against malfunctions associated with the acquisition of a new home?

    A.   Flood insurance
    B.   Homeowner's warranty insurance
    C.   HO2
    D.   Hazard insurance

37. What is it called when someone takes possession of a property without being the actual title holder?

    A.   Acceleration clause
    B.   Adverse possession
    C.   Easement
    D.   Escheat

38. What is a non-possessory interest in property or restrictive covenant burdening the title?

    A.   Adverse possession
    B.   Easement
    C.   Encumbrance
    D.   Escheat

39. What is the name given to the long beams that span the piers of a foundation offering support to the floor or ceiling?

    A.   Eaves
    B.   Frames
    C.   Joists
    D.   Studs

40. What conveys a grantor's interest in real property?

    A.   Agreement
    B.   Conveyance
    C.   Offering the loan
    D.   Title

41. What prohibits the solicitation of residential property listings?

    A. Commingling
    B. Non-solicitation order
    C. Regulation Z
    D. Termination of tenancy

42. What is exempt from property taxation?

    A. Colleges
    B. Office buildings
    C. Supermarkets
    D. Unoccupied land

43. Which fiduciary duty is violated by commingling?

    A. Accountability
    B. Disclosure
    C. Obedience
    D. Loyalty

44. What gives the government power to appropriate private property?

    A. Right of first refusal
    B. Riparian rights
    C. Eminent domain
    D. None of the above

45. What is the owner of a building prohibited to do regarding the disabled?

    A. Allow the disabled to be tenants
    B. Make the building accessible to the disabled
    C. Ensure they are treated like other tenants
    D. Refuse modifications for handicapped tenants

46. What act prohibits discrimination based on disability?

    A. The Americans with Disabilities Act of 1990
    B. Fair Housing Act
    C. Civil Rights Act of 1866
    D. Civil Right Act of 1964

47. What is the name given to a property tenure that can be terminated at any time?

    A. Tenancy in sufferance
    B. Terminated tenancy
    C. Tenancy in common
    D. Tenancy at will

48. If you have a loan of $350,000 with a 7% interest, how much do you pay in interest every month?

    A. $2,041
    B. $2,260
    C. $27,125
    D. $31,208

49. What law prohibits any type of discrimination on the basis of sex and gender?

   A. Fair Housing Act
   B. Civil Rights Act of 1866
   C. Civil Rights Act Amendment of 1974
   D. Americans with Disabilities Act

50. In 1988, the Civil Rights Act was amended to include?

   A. Married women
   B. Immigrants
   C. Black people
   D. Handicaps and familial status

51. What is the net income of a property valued at $500,000 and a capitalization rate of 14%?

   A. $70,000
   B. $43,000
   C. $840,000
   D. None of the above

52. What is the name of an appointed official who estimates the value of real property for taxing purposes?

   A. Agent
   B. Assessor
   C. Appraiser
   D. Tax official

53. What is the term used to describe a situation where a mortgage balance decreases due to periodic installments that pay down the principal and interest?

   A. Adjustable-rate mortgage
   B. Amortization
   C. Lock-in period
   D. Fixed-rate mortgage

54. What is an annual tax levied on the value of real property?

   A. Capital gains tax
   B. Real estate tax
   C. Progressive tax
   D. Regressive tax

55. What is the name given to a situation where an individual uses borrowed money to purchase a property?

   A. Buydown
   B. Purchase money
   C. Leverage
   D. Shorting

56. Which air conditioning system facilitates both heating and cooling?

   A. Forced air system
   B. Cooling system
   C. Heating system
   D. Thermostat

57. What is the waiting time for a real estate agent to renew a license once it is revoked?

    A. Two months
    B. One year
    C. Five years
    D. It is never reinstated

58. Who manages a co-op?

    A. Board of directors
    B. CEO
    C. Co-op developers
    D. Tenants

59. What is the value estimating process that uses similar available properties to determine the value of land?

    A. Mirror method
    B. Sales comparison method
    C. Allocation method
    D. Abstraction method

60. Who is required to sign a deed in a real estate transaction?

    A. Attorney
    B. Buyer
    C. Grantor
    D. Lender

61. What is a poisonous gas that comes from the breakdown of minerals in soil?

    A. Ammonia
    B. Chlorine
    C. Helium
    D. Radon

62. What are the rights of a person whose property is adjacent to or crossed by a river?

    A. Exclusive rights to sell
    B. Riparian rights
    C. Rights of first refusal
    D. Right of disclosure

63. What law requires full disclosure of all credit terms for consumer loans under the Truth in Lending Act?

    A. Americans with Disabilities Act
    B. Civil Rights Act
    C. Fair Housing Act
    D. Regulation Z

64. What is the name given to granting priority to an individual to buy or lease a property?

    A. Bundle of rights
    B. Exclusive right to sell
    C. Right of first refusal
    D. Right of possession

65. What is the loss of property value caused by economic or functional factors?

A. Economic obsolescence
B. Depreciation
C. Legal obsolescence
D. Aesthetic obsolescence

66. What kind of agent is a real estate agent?

A. Special agent
B. General agent
C. Dual agent
D. Subagent

67. What valuing method is Comparative Market Analysis **not** considered as?

A. Appraisal
B. Home valuing
C. Depreciation valuing
D. Tax returns valuing

68. What is a specific lien claimed by someone who has performed construction / repair / renovation work on the property and has **not** been paid?

A. Mechanic's lien
B. Involuntary lien
C. Mortgage
D. Judicial lien

69. What is the bottom piece of a frame that provides a nailing surface for the floor and wall system?

A. Eaves
B. Joist
C. Sill plate
D. Stud

70. What is a broker allowed to purchase for a real estate salesperson?

A. Phone
B. Medical insurance cover
C. Retirement plan
D. A company vehicle

71. When does a real estate salesperson first provide the agency disclosure form?

A. When the deal is about to be closed
B. After closing the deal
C. First substantial contact
D. Never

72. What is the definition of steering?

A. When you knowingly provide inaccurate information
B. Guiding families with children into an apartment building with other families with children and away from other buildings
C. Discriminating against people due to socio-economic status
D. Failing to provide proof of continuing real estate education

73. What is the value of a point on a mortgage?

    A. 1% of loan
    B. 5% of the loan
    C. 10% of the loan
    D. 50% of the loan

74. What type of talent are real estate salespeople?

    A. Assistants
    B. Independent contractors
    C. Part time employees
    D. Full time employees

75. What is the term used to describe a building that is separate from the main house?

    A. Supplemental structure
    B. Accessory building
    C. Secondary land
    D. Shed

76. The estate that provides absolute ownership of land is called?

    A. Fee simple estate
    B. Life estate
    C. Conditional fee estate
    D. Legal life estate

77. Which of the following is an example of community property?

    A. Property that is inherited by the husband through marriage
    B. Income that is earned by one spouse during the marriage
    C. Income earned prior to marriage
    D. A gift given to one spouse during the marriage

78. Fixture are considered _____.

    A. Hypothecation
    B. An agreement between the two parties
    C. Items that are removable by the tenant before the expiration date of the lease
    D. Real property

79. The commission that is due to a salesperson is decided by?

    A. Chattels
    B. State Law
    C. Mutual Agreement
    D. Court Decree

80. A real estate broker has become an agent of the seller when ____.

    A. A listing agreement with the seller has been executed
    B. They are responsible for sharing commissions
    C. A broker acts in good faith
    D. They are procuring cause

81. What is a promissory note?

    A.   An agreement between the mortgage company and borrower that shows the terms of the loan

    B.   A document that states the buyer's intention to buy a property for a specified amount

    C.   A note between the broker and buyer stating the exclusive-right-to-represent the buyer

    D.   An agreement between the seller and buyer providing a grace period for backing out of the sale

82. _____ occurs when a tenant vacates a premise because the landlord failed to provide essential services.

    A.   Quit notices

    B.   Actual eviction

    C.   Constructive eviction

    D.   Notice to quit

83. A buyer has _____ to cancel a contract if a Seller's Disclosure Notice has not been provided prior to the effective date of the contract.?

    A.   9 days

    B.   7 days

    C.   30 days

    D.   A Seller's Disclosure Notice is not necessary for buyers

84. Which is not true about the Federal Fair Housing Act?

    A.   Prohibits discrimination in housing due to age

    B.   Protects people from discrimination when renting or buying a home

    C.   Prohibits refusal to sell or rent a house due to familial status

    D.   All of the above

85. When a property loses value because of the lack of maintenance on natural wear and tear it is called _____.

    A. External depreciation
    B. Physical deterioration
    C. Economic obsolescence
    D. Negative amortization

86. Which of the following is an example of an appurtenance?

    A. Light bulbs
    B. Sofa
    C. Refrigerator
    D. Parking space

87. What is a syndicate?

    A. When one party operates a real estate investment
    B. When a party creates a real estate investment opportunity
    C. When two or more parties create and operate a real estate investment
    D. When a party builds a residential home for their family

88. Which of the following is a bundle of rights afforded to the buyer of real estate property?

    A. Right of control
    B. Right of exclusion
    C. Right of enjoyment
    D. All of the above

89. Which of the following is not a physical characteristic of land?

    A.   Immobility
    B.   Indestructability
    C.   Square footage
    D.   Uniqueness

90. A _____ is personal property that is used in a business and can be removed by the tenant when the lease ends.

    A.   Escheat
    B.   Trade fixtures
    C.   Plottage
    D.   Redlining

91. The _____ replaced dower and curtesy.

    A.   Uniform Probate Code
    B.   Real Estate Licensing Act
    C.   Real Estate Code of Conduct
    D.   Real Estate Code of Ethics

92. What is the highest possible ownership that can be held in real estate called?

    A.   Fee simple absolute
    B.   Estate at sufferance
    C.   Defeasible
    D.   Estate at will

93. Which of the following is an example of an encumbrance?

   A.   Student loans
   B.   Deed restriction
   C.   Mortgage
   D.   All of the above

94. The _____ determines the water usage in states where the water is scarce.

   A.   Property rights
   B.   Riparian rights
   C.   Doctrine Appropriation
   D.   Littoral rights

95. Which of the following is an example of a prescriptive easement?

   A.   Building a fence on a neighbor's property
   B.   Using a part of a neighbor's property to access the side of a road
   C.   A neighbor uses another neighbor's Wi-Fi
   D.   All of the above

96. A _____ is an interest in real property that is limited to the duration of the lifetime of the owner?

   A.   Life estate
   B.   Appurtenant easement
   C.   Deed restriction
   D.   Lien

97. This organization buys, owns and operates real estate for investors.

    A. National Investment Trust
    B. The Real Estate Investment Association
    C. Fair Housing Association
    D. Real Estate Investment Trust

98. Which tax is based on the value of real and personal property?

    A. Ad valorem tax
    B. Property tax
    C. Real estate tax
    D. Investment property tax

99. A _____ is a fixed object that is used as a permanent reference point to mark landownership boundaries.

    A. Datum
    B. Monument
    C. Metes and bounds
    D. Nonhomogeneity

100. What is a chain or title?

    A. A history of ownership regarding a property's title
    B. A line from which elevations are measured
    C. A comparison of homes sold in the same area
    D. The right a broker has to collect commission even if the property is not sold

THIS IS THE END OF THE NATIONAL PORTION.

State Portion

1. A provisional broker is required to completed _____ of post licensing education in North Carolina.

   A. 75 hours
   B. 90 hours
   C. 50 hours
   D. 120 hours

2. North Carolina requires licensees to carry their _____ when engaging in real estate.

   A. Pocket card
   B. Business card
   C. Identification card
   D. Brokerage information

3. A licensee is required to complete continuing education, some of those hours of education are general updates. What do the other hours consist of?

   A. Legal course
   B. Selling information
   C. Contracts education
   D. Elective education

4. A license is expired if the licensee _____.

   A. Fails to renew the license
   B. Does not sell more than 20 houses a year
   C. Fails to pay the renewal fee
   D. A&C only

5. Which of the following must a provisional broker do to activate a license?

A. Sell 1 home
B. Move to broker status
C. Affiliate with a broker in charge
D. All of the above

6. To renew a license that has been expired for less than 6 months, what does the licensee have to do?

A. Renew late
B. Pay an additional fee
C. Retake the licensee exam
D. A&B only

7. What is the rescission period for a new condominium purchased in North Carolina?

A. 7 days
B. 2 days
C. 10 days
D. 5 days

8. All time-share projects must be _____ according to the North Carolina Timeshares Act.

A. Paid a development fee
B. Taxed by usage
C. Registered with the state
D. All of the above

9. According to the North Carolina Timeshares Act, the purchaser of a new timeshare has a _____ rescission period.

   A. 7 day
   B. 2 day
   C. 10 day
   D. 5 day

10. An approved lien agent is required when a property owner applies for a building permit for improvements totaling more than _____.

   A. $30,000
   B. $10,000
   C. $50,000
   D. $25,000

11. A broker sells a home, but the principal does not pay the commission owed to the broker. Which of the following can a broker do to collect unpaid commissions?

   A. Report them to NCREC
   B. Place a lien on the property
   C. Cancel the sale of the home
   D. All of the above

12. The developer of a time share must file an affidavit with the _____.

   A. County clerk's office
   B. NCREC
   C. Governor
   D. Federal Government

13. The North Carolina Condominium Act of 1985 requires the developer to provide which form to buyers?

    A. Condominium insurance forms
    B. Public offering statement
    C. Past public sales documents
    D. None of the above

14. Which statement is true about expired licenses in North Carolina?

    A. The broker with the expired license can complete jobs already begun when the license was active
    B. The broker with the expired license cannot earn commission or referral fees
    C. The broker with the expired license can take on clients if there is intention on reactivating the license
    D. None of the above is true

15. This strip of land that is part of the shore between the high and low tide lines is the _____, and belongs to the state of North Carolina.

    A. Riparian land
    B. Littoral land
    C. Foreshore
    D. Public property

16. Property owners, in North Carolina, whose land is bordered by the ocean or a large navigable lake that has a tide, owns the land adjacent to the water up to the _____.

    A. They do not own this property it is owned by the state
    B. End of the land where it meets the ocean
    C. Mean high-water mark
    D. Property owners cannot own land that borders an ocean

17. In order for a manufactured home to become real property in North Carolina, the home must have the _____ removed and the unit must be attached to a permanent foundation.

  A. Moving hitch
  B. Wheels
  C. Axles
  D. All of the above

18. In North Carolina, agricultural fixtures are considered _____.

  A. Private property
  B. Real property
  C. Public property
  D. Governmental property

19. Which law states that if a homeowner purchases an item on credit and gives the creditor a security agreement, then the item is considered personal property until it is paid in full?

  A. North Carolina Uniform Commercial Code (UCC)
  B. Real Property Law
  C. Federal Creditor Act
  D. North Carolina Property Act

20. In North Carolina, only a husband and wife can create a _____, by deed or by will.

  A. Joint tenancy
  B. Tenancy by the entirety
  C. Right of survivorship
  D. Deed of trust

21. The North Carolina Condominium Act of 1986 states that the condominium developer must file a _____.

   A. Plat map
   B. Request to build
   C. Financial plan
   D. Affidavit

22. A provisional broker has an expired license for 1 year, the broker would like to begin practicing law again. What does the provisional broker have to do?

   A. Write a statement explaining why they let the license expire and why the commission should allow the licensee to practice again
   B. Take additional education
   C. Retake the provisional broker licensing test
   D. All of the above

23. The North Carolina Commercial Real Estate Broker Lien law allows a broker _____ after tenant possession to file the lien.

   A. 90 days
   B. 60 days
   C. 180 days
   D. 30 days

24. North Carolina requires a deed to be _____ in order for it to be valid.

   A. Signed by a witness
   B. In writing
   C. Notarized
   D. Verbal

25. The excise tax is valid for all property sales except transfers of conveyances by _____.

   A. A government entity
   B. A will
   C. Intestate succession due to death
   D. All of the above

26. A _____ is recognized as a method of condemnation when authorized by law, in the state of North Carolina.

   A. Public take
   B. Quick domain
   C. Quick take
   D. None of the above

27. If the adverse possessor has a color of title, continuous possession is required for _____, for adverse possession in North Carolina.

   A. 7 years
   B. 10 years
   C. 5 years
   D. 15 years

28. The North Carolina _____ states that a court appoints an administrator or administratrix to distribute the deceased person's property.

   A. Machinery Act
   B. Intestate Succession Act
   C. Condominium Act
   D. Timeshare Act

29. North Carolina is a(n) _____, which means that title searches are usually performed by an attorney.

   A. Approved attorney state
   B. Legal title search state
   C. State approved title state
   D. None of the above

30. In North Carolina, this act states that if a person has who has been vested with any estate in real property for 30 years or more, shall have a marketable record title.

   A. Federal title act
   B. Marketable title act
   C. Real estate marketable title act
   D. None of the above

31. Which of the following is required of the grantor in order to convey title to real estate?

   A. Grantor must have legal existence
   B. Be of lawful age
   C. Be legally competent
   D. All of the above

32. A _____ must be paid by all sellers of real property in the state of North Carolina.

   A. Broker commission
   B. Sales tax
   C. Excise tax
   D. Real estate tax

33. A property owner who dies intestate with no next of kin, the property will _____ to the state.

    A.   Arbitrate
    B.   Escheat
    C.   Blocklist
    D.   Quick take

34. Which of the following trumps intestate succession laws?

    A.   Right of survivorship
    B.   Tenancy of the entirety
    C.   Will
    D.   None of the above trumps intestate succession laws

35. The _____ statute states that whoever records the deed first prevails.

    A.   First deed statute
    B.   Race state
    C.   Pure race statute
    D.   First come first serve statute

36. This act requires many types of real estate documents to be recorded for protection against claims of third parties.

    A.   North Carolina Connor Act
    B.   The Lay Act
    C.   North Carolina Real Estate Act
    D.   None of the above

37. The title insurance company issues a _____ based on the opinion on title.

    A. Sales insurance
    B. Title commitment
    C. Deed
    D. Deed insurance

38. Which of the following is required for a deed to be valid in the state of North Carolina?

    A. Contain an accurate legal description
    B. Signed by the grantors
    C. Legal capacity to execute a deed
    D. All of the above

39. An example of a(n) _____ is a utility company running a power line across a burdened piece of property. In North Carolina, this is viewed as a personal right and irrevocable during the owner's life.

    A. Easement in gross
    B. Appurtenant easement
    C. Negative easement
    D. None of the above

40. The North Carolina Commercial Real Estate Broker Lien law states that the lien must be satisfied within 18 months and is inferior to a _____.

    A. Judgement lien
    B. Mechanic's lien
    C. Judicial lien
    D. Statutory lien

THIS IS THE END OF THE STATE PORTION.

Answer Key – National Portion

1.	C	21.	D	41.	B	61.	D	81.	A
2.	A	22.	A	42.	A	62.	B	82.	C
3.	D	23.	C	43.	A	63.	D	83.	B
4.	A	24.	D	44.	C	64.	C	84.	A
5.	C	25.	D	45.	D	65.	A	85.	B
6.	B	26.	A	46.	A	66.	A	86.	D
7.	D	27.	A	47.	D	67.	A	87.	C
8.	C	28.	A	48.	A	68.	A	88.	D
9.	C	29.	B	49.	C	69.	C	89.	C
10.	B	30.	A	50.	D	70.	A	90.	B
11.	C	31.	B	51.	A	71.	C	91.	A
12.	C	32.	A	52.	B	72.	B	92.	A
13.	A	33.	B	53.	B	73.	A	93.	B
14.	A	34.	B	54.	B	74.	B	94.	C
15.	A	35.	A	55.	C	75.	B	95.	B
16.	B	36.	B	56.	A	76.	A	96.	A
17.	B	37.	B	57.	B	77.	B	97.	D
18.	C	38.	C	58.	A	78.	D	98.	A
19.	C	39.	C	59.	D	79.	C	99.	B
20.	A	40.	B	60.	C	80.	A	100.	A

1. **C) Foreclosure**

This is the legal process where a lender seeks to recover the balance of a loan by selling the property held as collateral. Foreclosure usually occurs after a lender has legally obtained a termination of the borrower's right of redemption.

2. **A) Asbestos**

Asbestos is a naturally occurring mineral and its insulation qualities make it popular in making fireproof materials. When products containing asbestos are disturbed, they release tiny fibers in the air that when inhaled over a long period of time can be detrimental as they accumulate in the lung causing scarring and inflammation. Continued exposure affects cells resulting in a rare cancer known as mesothelioma.

3. **D) Studs**

These are vertical beams that are used during construction to frame the house. They are used to form or position walls in a building. Previously, studs made of timber dominated the construction industry but modern construction styles have embraced the use of steel.

4.   **A) Misrepresentation**

Misrepresentation occurs when a broker misstates information of property. It is a false statement that may affect a person's decision to enter into a contract. Three types of misrepresentation are fraudulent misrepresentation, negligent misrepresentation and innocent misrepresentation.

5.   **C) Preventive maintenance**

In order to maintain tenants and an acceptable return on an investment, routine checks and repairs have to be done. These are done to safeguard against failing which may incur losses to the property manager that arise due to cost of replacement.

6.   **B) Mortgagee**

A mortgagee is an entity that lends money for the purpose of buying a real estate property. As a precaution, the mortgagee establishes prior interest in the property and maintains the title as collateral.

7.   **D) $156,250**

$150,000 / (1 - 0.04) = $156,250

8.   **C) Land zoning**

This refers to the restriction of physical development and the use of certain parcels of land. It is done with regard to zoning laws and purposes to protect wildlife and natural resources. It is also used to restrict the number of domestic animals that can be accommodated on a property.

9.   **C) Initiate judicial foreclosure**

Judicial foreclosure are court proceedings that allow the lender to seize the property that was held as collateral for sale. This is done in order to regain the principal amount. This can only be done once it has been established that a defaulting borrower is unable to continue making payments

10.   **B) CERCLA**

This is a trade association that is aimed at trying to improve oversight by representing title insurance. It considers a mortgage a high risk and therefore title insurance must be taken to protect lender

11. **C) Fair Credit Reporting Act**

Credit reporting is the process of collecting and analyzing consumers credit information by credit bureaus. This information is sold to lending facilities in order to help them determine whether or not a borrower is eligible for a loan. This act was passed to highlight consumer rights when it comes to credit information.

12. **C) Right of egress**

This is the legal right granted to homeowners as they allow access to property. These rights are usually obtained through an easement and apply regardless of the property type.

13. **A) Sweat equity**

This is the non-monetary equity that owners contribute into the business or property. In this case, sweat equity is the amount of effort an owner puts into a property in order to increase its value.

14. **A) Buydown**

This is a mortgage-financing technique that allows a borrower to negotiate lower monthly payment rates. It usually involves the seller making payments to the lending institution to reduce monthly payment rate of the buyer. As a result, the purchase price goes up.

15. **A) Clear title**

A clear title is a title that has no liens or levies from creditors and other involved parties. A clear title is used to ensure there is no question of ownership. It shows that there are no outstanding financial responsibilities attached to the property and the owner is legally capable of selling the property.

16. **B) Credit report**

A credit report is a detailed breakdown of an individual's credit history and is usually carried out by credit bureaus. They use financial information attached to an individual like their bill payment to establish a unique report. This information is usually used by lenders while considering a loan applicant.

17. **B) Equity**

Equity is another term for ownership. In home investments, equity means the amount of principal that has been paid off. The higher the equity the easier it is to refinance a property.

18. **C) Notice of default**

This is a public notice filed in court regarding a borrower's default on a loan. It is usually to notify the borrower that there has been a breach in the contractual limit that had been predetermined in the loan. A grace period is included for negotiation before further action is considered.

19. **C) Lock-in period**

This is the period usually 30 to 60 days within which a lender is required to keep a loan offer open. This gives the borrower enough time to prepare for closing while the lender is processing the loan. A lock in period protects the borrower from losses incurred throughout the repayment of the loan caused by rising interest rates during processing of the loan.

20. **A) When a tenant breaks a rent prior to the date of expiry without a legal reason**

As a lease is a contract, breaking a lease without a valid reason may result in being sued by the landlord. To avoid legal action, the individual breaking the lease must prove beyond reasonable doubt that the break was caused by a situation completely out of their hands.

21. **D) Shortfall**

Shortfall is a term used to describe a situation where a financial obligation exceeds the required amount of cash available. A shortfall may be a temporary and current situation or a prolonged one. The latter represents mismanagement of funds and warrants a deeper look into spending habits and change has to be implemented.

22. **A) Tax abatement**

Tax abatement is a strategy used by the government to increase investments in specific areas. In the real estate sector, tax abatement occurs when taxes on properties are significantly reduced or completely eliminated. It is usually done to encourage investors to buy property in areas that have recorded long term low demand.

23. **C) $546,000**

$500,000 * 1.04 * 1.05 = $546,000

24. **D) Department of Health**

25. **D) $368,000**

$92,000 / 0.25 = $368,000

26.	**A) Abstract of title**

This is a summarized history of all title transfers and legal actions that have been connected with a certain property. It is beneficial in preventing home buyers from getting tangled in legal issues that are attached to a property. This is because any loss made because of a court ruling on a property once a buyer has purchased will be incurred by the new tenant.

27.	**A) Flashing**

This is a material used to cover joints where two or more types of material join. This usually happens to prevent water leakage through the joint. It also provides a drainage between two joints.

28.	**A) Eaves**

This is a part of the roof that projects over the wall beyond the edge of the roof. It is usually set in place to channel water away from the roof.

29.	**B) Cash on cash return**

Cash on cash return that a proven metric used to calculate future cash returns on a cash investment. This metric is only true for a cash investment and does not take into account loan investments.

30.	**A) Architectural Review Board**

The Architectural Review Board is given the responsibility of upholding the visual integrity of a town. It is responsible for reviewing all exterior designs of all residential and commercial structures in a town. All new structures and structures that are up for alteration are required to provide a blueprint of the exterior design for printing. They are also charged with ensuring commercial signs conform to the towns design.

31.	**B) Gross lease**

A gross lease is a lease where a flat rent fee is paid. It includes rent and other utility fees such as taxes and insurance. A landlord is obligated to calculate a rate based on history or research. A negotiation between the tenant and landlord can also be reached on the services the tenant wants to be included in the lease.

32.	**A) House rules**

These are rules that are given to tenants of a coop or condo on the beginning of the contract regarding behavior within the complex. They are put in place to ensure a comfortable living space for all occupants. Failure to adhere to the rules may result in eviction.

33.   **B) Absorption rate**

This is a ration of the number of properties that have been sold against the number of properties that are available for sale within a specified area.

34.   **B) Acceleration clause**

This is a provision in a mortgage that allows the lender the right to demand the immediate settlement on a mortgage under certain predetermined conditions such as a borrower defaulting on a loan.

35.   **A) Easement appurtenant**

Easement appurtenant is an agreement that is transferable with ownership rights of a property. When a property is transferred through sale or inheritance, all rights and privileges attached to the land are automatically transferred to the new owner.

36.   **B) Homeowner's warranty insurance**

Homeowner's warranty insurance insures the homeowner from the builder's faults for a specified warranty period

37.   **B) Adverse possession**

This is a legal principle that allows a person who has been living on a specific land for a long period of time to take possession of the land without permission of the owner. The individual does not have to have a title to the land to acquire it. The title holder is capable of claiming his land by choosing to eject the squatter.

38.   **C) Encumbrance**

This is a limitation against a real estate property. It restricts the owner from transferring ownership of the title. It also prevents an owner from depreciating the value of the property.

39.   **C) Joists**

These are horizontal structural members used to frame an open space. They are often used in transferring loads to the vertical members of the structure. When used in floors, they provide stiffness in the framing systems.

40.   **B) Conveyance**

A conveyance or sale deed is a legally binding contract that transfers all ownership rights from the seller to the buyer. It usually states the agreed-on price, the date of the transaction and the obligations of the parties involved.

41.   **B) Non-solicitation order**

This is an order issued to broker and agents to prevent them from soliciting listings in designated areas

42.   **A) Colleges**

Despite the fact that all property is assessed to determine its value, universities, schools, parks, government institutions, religious organizations, and hospitals are exempt from property taxes. Veterans are also eligible from partial exemption from taxes.

43.   **A) Accountability**

Commingling is a contract breach where a fiduciary mixed funds belonging to a client with his own making it impossible to separate them. The accountability clause requires a fiduciary to be able to maintain an accurate report of documents and funds that he/she has been entrusted.

44.   **C) Eminent domain**

This is the government's power to take private land for public use under certain circumstances. It is defined by the Taking Clause of the Fifth Amendment which prohibits the taking of private land without just compensation. It emphasizes that the government can only take land for public use and offer just compensation on the land.

45.   **D) Refuse modifications for handicapped tenants**

Refuse to allow tenants to make reasonable structural modifications to a unit at the tenant's expense to allow the handicapped tenant full enjoyment of the property (Fair Housing Act). In accordance with the Fair Housing Act which is against discrimination in housing, multifamily buildings are expected to ensure accessibility for people using wheelchairs

46.   **A) The Americans with Disabilities Act of 1990**

This act was enacted to ensure disabled people are not discriminated against and have equal rights regarding access to employment and commercial facilities.

47.   **D) Tenancy at will**

This is a tenancy that is not bound by a lease and does not have an expiry or duration of tenancy. A predetermined payment plan is adhered and a tenant is flexible to terminate the tenancy without legal proceedings. It is a beneficial plan for landlords and tenants that seek flexibility.

48.   **A) $2,041**

($350,000 * 0.07) / 12 = $2,041

49.   **C) Civil Rights Act Amendment of 1974**

The Civil Rights act amendment of 1974 banned discrimination based on sex and credit in a congress proceeding. Women being offered maternity leave on the assumption that they were unable to work was rendered illegal and sexist teaching methods were discredited.

50.   **D) Handicaps and familial status**

The act protects people with disabilities and families with children. Pregnant women were also protected from illegal discrimination.

51.   **A) $70,000**

$500,000 * 0.14 = $70,000

52.   **B) Assessor**

An assessor is a government official that is engaged to determine the value of a property. The information gathered by an assessor is used to calculate future property taxes. Assessors maintain annual assessments at a uniform percentage of market value.

53.   **B) Amortization**

This is the scheduling of monthly mortgage payments showing breakdown of payment. When paying a mortgage loan for a property, the initial payments are put towards paying off the interest and less is allocated to the principal amount. As a borrower makes more payments, more is allocated to the principal and less to the interest.

54.   **B) Real estate tax**

This is an ad valorem tax on the value of a property. It is levied annually on real estate by the government authority.

55.   **C) Leverage**

This refers to money that has been borrowed to finance an investment property. The leverage concept works best when rent and property values are on the rise. Monthly mortgage payments for the rental property become constant which results in a rise in profits

56.   **A) Forced air system**

A forced air system refers to any HVAC system that makes use of air ducts and vents to release temperature-controlled air into the building. A forced air system released filtered and dehumidified cold air into buildings and runs at an affordable price. A central air system on the other hand uses vents in the forced air system to provide cool and conditioned air.

57. **B) One year**

An individual is required to wait for an entire year after which the agent is required to prove with evidence that he/she is capable of being trustworthy and upholding the law with regard to the real estate sector.

58. **A) Board of directors**

A co-op is an alternative method to traditional housing. A board of directors is elected by the shareholders to run the corporation. They are responsible for vetting and doing background checks on potential new shareholders in the corporation. They are also responsible for upholding the values and regulations of the co-op and terminating tenancy of individuals found to be acting contrary to the rules.

59. **D) Abstraction method**

This is a method of estimating the value of a piece of land that is based on the going price of similar parcels of land within the area.

60. **C) Grantor**

This is the party that transfers ownership of property to buyer through a legal document known as a deed. The grantor is required to sign the deed admitting the transfer of ownership before closing. The deed is then filed at the county jurisdiction for public record.

61. **D) Radon**

Radon is a radioactive cancer-causing gas that comes from the natural breakdown of uranium in soil. The gas penetrates its way into houses from cracks and holes in the foundation. Testing for radon gas is mandatory during purchasing of a home in order to fix the problem by lowering the amount of radon gas available to the acceptable amounts.

62. **B) Riparian rights**

These are rights that arise when an individual owns land near a moving watercourse. These rights include swimming and irrigation. The rights only attach when there's a water on one side of the land. An individual is allowed to benefit from the water body without contaminating or altering the flow of the waterbody.

63. **D) Regulation Z**

It requires lenders to make comprehensive disclosure statements to borrowers for consumer loans. It is aimed at protecting consumers from misleading lending practices. Lenders are required to disclose interest rates, finance charges, explain terms used and respond to all complaints launched by the borrower. This law was passed to ensure that borrowers make informed credit choices.

64. **C) Right of first refusal**

This is the right given to a specific party to purchase or lease a property before it is open to bidding by other potential buyers. The party being offered the privilege is not obligated to buy the property. In the event that the party is not interested in the property, it is opened up to the public.

65. **A) Economic obsolescence**

This is the decrease in the market value of a property due to external factors that cannot be controlled by the property owner i.e. building of an interstate highway close to a prime property. Its value immediately decreases due to the noise pollution.

66. **A) Special agent**

A special agent is an agent whose services are only employed for a specific task. Once the task is completed a special agent no longer has authority to represent the client.

67. **A) Appraisal**

An appraisal in a professional opinion value assessment of a property and is independent of the market values of similar properties based on the fact that all properties are unique and cannot be compared to each other.

68. **A) Mechanic's lien**

This is a security interest in title of property for the benefit of those who supplied materials and offered professional services on the construction and renovation of a property. A mechanic's lien can be taken on both real and personal properties.

69. **C) Sill plate**

This is a horizontal member of a wall where vertical members of the building are attached. It usually lies between the foundation and floor frame.

70. **A) Phone**

This is because salespeople are considered independent contractors and therefore are not eligible for company benefits.

71. **C) First substantial contact**

This refers to the earliest practicable opportunity during a conversation with the consumer. An agency disclosure is to be provided to disclose and explain the nature of the representation in a real estate transaction.

72. **B) Guiding families with children into an apartment building with other families with children and away from other buildings**

Steering is an unlawful practice that violates the federal fair housing provisions. It is a practice in which brokers influence the choice of a prospective buyer or tenant.

73. **A) 1% of loan**

A value point is a fee paid directly to the lender at closing in exchange for a reduced interest rate and can lower a borrower's monthly mortgage payment.

74. **B) Independent contractors**

Independent contractors are hired to perform a service but are not included in the employee catalogue. Their main goal is to complete the task and the employing broker has no control over the process of yielding results or financial expenses incurred.

75. **B) Accessory building**

This is a building that is built separately from the main structure in a property. It is usually put to use for a specific purpose such as a shed, workshop or garage.

76. **A) Fee simple estate**

This provides absolute ownership of the land and allows the owner to do whatever they choose to with the land. This is the highest form of ownership in real estate.

77. **B) Income that is earned by one spouse during the marriage**

Community property is defined as everything that a married couple owns together. This includes income and property acquired during the duration of the marriage.

78. **D) Real property**

A fixture is physically property that is permanently attached to real property (on it or under it), that cannot be moved. Examples include ponds, canals, buildings and roads.

79. **C) Mutual Agreement**

An agreement between a buyer and a seller. It is a binding contract between the two parties and includes any contingencies.

80. **A) A listing agreement with the seller has been executed**

A listing agreement is a contract between the homeowner and a selling agent. It is a legal agreement that gives the selling agent the right to sell the home.

81.   **A) An agreement between the mortgage company and borrower that shows the terms of the loan**

This binding note states the terms of the loan and that the borrower promises to for the loan. It also provides evidence of the loan and both parties must sign the note to make it legally binding.

82.   **C) Constructive eviction**

A constructive eviction is when a tenant must move out because the landlord fails to do something which renders the property uninhabitable. The tenant needs to give notice of the condition and allow a reasonable amount of time for the landlord to fix it. If this does not occur, the tenant can move out.

83.   **B) 7 days**

If a seller's disclosure notice is not provided to the buyer, then they buyer has 7 days to cancel the contract.

84.   **A) Prohibits discrimination in housing due to age**

The Federal Fair Housing Law prohibits discrimination due to race, color, national origin, religion, sex, familiar status and disability. This act prohibits discrimination when renting or buying a home, getting a mortgage, seeking housing assistance or engaging in other housing-related activities.

85.   **B) Physical deterioration**

This is the most obvious form of depreciation and can occur when maintenance does not keep up with natural wear and tear. It causes a loss of value to the property. There are two types of physical deterioration functional obsolescence and external obsolescence.

86.   **D) Parking space**

Appurtenances are real property that is immovable or fixed to the land. Parking spaces and water rights are considered an appurtenance.

87.   **C) When two or more parties create and operate a real estate investment**

A syndicate is when investors pool their financial and intellectual resources to invest in real estate properties. These investments are bigger than a party would be able to afford individually.

88.   **D) All of the above**

The right of disposition is also a bundle of rights. It is a set of legal privileges that affords a real estate buyer when the transfer of title occurs.

89.   **C) Square footage**

Land has three characteristics, immobility, indestructibility and uniqueness. Some of the characteristics are immovable and can be changed, but location is an immobile characteristic.

90.   **B) Trade fixtures**

Trade fixtures are removable personal property that is attached by the tenant to a leased land for the purpose of business i.e. display county. The trade fixture must be removable without damage to the property.

91.   **A) Uniform Probate Code**

The Uniform Probate Code states that when a spouse dies the surviving spouse can take an elective share on the death of their spouse. It is an act that was drafted by the National Conference of Commissioners on Uniform State Laws.

92.   **A) Fee simple absolute**

The fee simple absolute is the maximum possible right of ownership in real property. It is a form of freehold ownership and continues forever.

93.   **B) Deed restrictions**

An encumbrance is a limitation or liability against real estate. A lien, deed restriction, easements, encroachments and licenses are all encumbrances. It restricts the owner's ability to transfer the property title.

94.   **C) Doctrine of Appropriation**

The Doctrine of Appropriation says that water rights are determined by priority of beneficial use. The first person to use water or divert the water for beneficial purposes can acquire the individual rights to the water.

95.   **B) Using a part of a neighbor's property to access the side of a road**

Prescriptive easement is when the right to use another's land is acquired through continued use without permission. There are three different types of easement: easement in gross, easement appurtenant and prescriptive easement. Regulations differ from state to state.

96. **A) Life estate**

A life estate lasts the duration of a person's life. It is also called a life tenancy. The estate in real property ends at the death and ownership of the property reverts back to the original owner.

97. **D) Real Estate Investment Trust**

This company owns and operates income-producing real estate. REIT owns commercial property such as apartment buildings, warehouses, hospitals and shopping centers.

98. **A) Ad valorem tax**

The ad valorem tax is based on the value of the property. It is imposed at the time of a transaction just like a value-added tax.

99. **B) Monument**

A natural or manmade, fixed object that is used as a reference point for surveying land. It is a tangible landmark that has been established to indicate a boundary.

100. **A) A history of ownership regarding a property's title**

A chain of title goes back to the original owner of the property and is the sequence of historical transfers of title. A chain of title search typically goes back 40 years to ensure there are no defects.

Answer Key – State Portion

1.	B	21.	A
2.	A	22.	B
3.	D	23.	A
4.	D	24.	B
5.	C	25.	D
6.	D	26.	C
7.	A	27.	A
8.	C	28.	B
9.	D	29.	A
10.	A	30.	B
11.	B	31.	D
12.	B	32.	C
13.	B	33.	B
14.	B	34.	A
15.	C	35.	C
16.	C	36.	A
17.	D	37.	B
18.	B	38.	D
19.	A	39.	A
20.	B	40.	B

1. **B) 90 hours**

The provisional broker needs to finish 90 hours of post-licensing education. This education must be completed within 3 years of obtaining a license.

2. **A) Pocket card**

The licensee must carry a pocket card when engaging in real estate. A pocket card is a pocket-sized real estate license that is issue to brokers and salespersons and identifies a licensee.

3. **D) Elective education**

The licensee is required to completed 8 hours of continuing education each year. 4 of those hours are general updates and the rest of those hours are elective courses.

4. **D) A&C only**

The licensee must pay the fee or fails to renew their license. This may also happen if the fee is dishonored by the bank.

5. **C) Affiliate with a broker in charge**

The provisional licensee must affiliate with a broker in charge in order to have their real estate license activated. The broker in charge must file the activation form for the provision licensee.

6. **D) A&B only**

The licensee must do a late renewal and they are required to pay an additional fee for the licensee to be in good standing and practice real estate again.

7. **A) 7 days**

The North Carolina Condominium Act states that the buyer of a new condominium has 7 days to rescind the offer. The rescission period typically begins when the public offering statement is given.

8. **C) Registered with the state**

The Timeshares Act requires time-share projects to be registered with the state of North Carolina. It also requires developers to provide public offering statements to buyers.

9. **D) 5 day**

While condominiums have a 7-day rescission period, time shares in the state of North Carolina have a 5 days rescission period.

10. **A) $30,000**

An approved lien agent for the project is required for improvement totaling more than 30,000 dollars. This includes all private and residential construction projects except projects for single-family detached property.

11. **B) Place a lien on the property**

The North Carolina Commercial Real Estate Broker Lien law allows for real estate agents to do this in order to gain commissions not paid.

12. **B) NCREC**

Developers of time-shares in the state of North Carolina must file an affidavit with the commission.

13. **B) Public offering statement**

This document is provided to the buyers of a new condominium by the developer. It contains details regarding the condominium structure and management as well as disclosures regarding budgets, insurance, construction, and rules.

14. **B) The broker with the expired license cannot earn commission or referral fees**

If the licensee has an expired license, they cannot earn commission or referral fees after the expiration. If there are fee unpaid from when their license was active, the individual has a right to those fees.

15. **C) Foreshore**

A foreshore is land that borders the ocean between the high and low tide lines. This land is not private property and is owned by the state.

16. **C) Mean high-water mark**

The mean high-water mark is a point representative of the maximum rise of a body of water over land.

17. **D) All of the above**

In order for the manufactured home to become real property, the home needs to have the moving hitch, axles and wheels removed. The property also needs to be permanently attached to the property. The owner is also required to file an affidavit

18. **B) Real property**

Agricultural fixtures are article that have been annexed for the purpose of farming and are considered real property in North Carolina.

19. **A) North Carolina Uniform Commercial Code**

This law is a method of providing notice of a security interest in personal property to interested third parties. It adopted the notice filing system.

20. **B) Tenancy by the entirety**

This is a hybrid of common law and statutory law. Its basic elements are that it can only exist between husband and wife and those not husband and wife cannot own real property through tenancy by the entirety.

21.   **A) Plat map**

This act requires the condominium developers to file a plat map or a plan of the condominium property, buildings, and any other improvements.

22.   **B) Take additional education**

In this case, the provisional broker has an expired license for more than 6 months so in order for the licensee to have an active license, the licensee must reapply, pay for another background check, and complete additional education.

23.   **A) 90 days**

This lien law gives a broker 90 days to file a lien against a property to be sold or leased to protect the brokers commission.

24.   **B) In writing**

North Carolina requires a deed to be in writing in order for it to be valid. A deed is a legal document that transfers ownership from the seller to the buyer.

25.   **D) All of the above**

Conveyances transferred by a government entity, by a will or intestate succession due to death, by a deed of gift with no consideration of payment, by merger are all exempt from the excise tax. Transfer to secure debt is also exempt.

26.   **C) Quick take**

A quick take gives a condemning authority the right to immediately take possession of property once the judgement is granted in its favor.

27.   **A) 7 years**

The claimant must also show actual, open, hostile, exclusive, and continuous possession of the land. They must have continuous possession for 7 years.

28.   **B) Intestate Succession Act**

The provisions of this act states that a court appoints a person to distribute the deceased's property. This person is called an administrator or administratrix.

29.   **A) Approved attorney state**

An approved attorney state is a state on the east coast that requires real estate attorneys to be actively involved in closing transactions.

30. **B) Marketable title act**

This act states that if a chain of title can be traced back for 30 years with no other claim being recorded during that title, the title becomes marketable.

31. **D) All of the above**

All of the above is required for a grantor to convey title to real estate.

32. **C) Excise tax**

This is an internal tax that is levied on the sale of specific goods and services. For real estate, the tax is based on the sale price of the property.

33. **B) Escheat**

Escheat is the concept of a piece of real property lacking appropriate ownership and the act of transferring ownership of the property to the reigning governmental agency.

34. **A) Right of survivorship**

Right of survivorship or joint ownership is the right that the surviving owner automatically owns the property when the owner dies.

35. **C) Pure race statute**

This statute states that if the purchaser fails to record a deed but a second purchaser does record a deed then the subsequent purchaser's title takes precedence over the first purchaser's title.

36. **A) North Carolina Connor Act**

The documents covered in this act include deeds, mortgages, installment land contracts, assignments, options, leases longer than 3 years, easements, and restrictive covenants.

37. **B) Title commitment**

The attorney is required to submit a preliminary opinion on title to the end title insurance company which serves as an application for the title insurance.

38. **D) All of the above**

A valid deed requires a legal description, signed by the grantors, and must have the legal capacity to execute the deed. It must also be delivered and voluntarily accepted by the grantee.

39. **A) Easement in gross**

An easement in gross is the legal right to use another person's land for the length of the owner's life. It terminates on the death of the personal easement owner.

40. **B) Mechanic's lien**

This lien is inferior to all mechanic's liens, and the tenant must satisfy the lien within 18 months.

Practice Test 3

Directions:

1.   You have a 4-hour time limit to complete the whole exam.

2.   To pass, you must answer at least 71 out of 100 questions correctly on the national portion **AND** at least 29 out of 40 questions on the state portion.

3.   Some questions will require mathematics. You may use a calculator.

4.   **Phones and pagers are not allowed. Having either will result in automatic dismissal from the exam and nullification of exam scores.**

Tips:

- Answer all questions even if you are unsure.
- Mark any questions you are stuck on and revisit them after you are done. The exam is timed so make sure you finish as many questions as you can.
- After reading the question, try answering it in your head first to avoid getting confused by the choices.
- Read the entire question before looking at the answers.
- Use the process of elimination to filter out choices that don't seem correct to increase your chances of selecting the correct answer.
- Be aware of important keywords like **not, sometimes, always,** and **never**. These words completely alter the ask of the question so it's important to keep track of them.

PLEASE READ THESE INSTRUCTIONS CAREFULLY.

Name: _____   Date: _____

NATIONAL PORTION

1. Ⓐ Ⓑ Ⓒ Ⓓ	31. Ⓐ Ⓑ Ⓒ Ⓓ	61. Ⓐ Ⓑ Ⓒ Ⓓ	91. Ⓐ Ⓑ Ⓒ Ⓓ
2. Ⓐ Ⓑ Ⓒ Ⓓ	32. Ⓐ Ⓑ Ⓒ Ⓓ	62. Ⓐ Ⓑ Ⓒ Ⓓ	92. Ⓐ Ⓑ Ⓒ Ⓓ
3. Ⓐ Ⓑ Ⓒ Ⓓ	33. Ⓐ Ⓑ Ⓒ Ⓓ	63. Ⓐ Ⓑ Ⓒ Ⓓ	93. Ⓐ Ⓑ Ⓒ Ⓓ
4. Ⓐ Ⓑ Ⓒ Ⓓ	34. Ⓐ Ⓑ Ⓒ Ⓓ	64. Ⓐ Ⓑ Ⓒ Ⓓ	94. Ⓐ Ⓑ Ⓒ Ⓓ
5. Ⓐ Ⓑ Ⓒ Ⓓ	35. Ⓐ Ⓑ Ⓒ Ⓓ	65. Ⓐ Ⓑ Ⓒ Ⓓ	95. Ⓐ Ⓑ Ⓒ Ⓓ
6. Ⓐ Ⓑ Ⓒ Ⓓ	36. Ⓐ Ⓑ Ⓒ Ⓓ	66. Ⓐ Ⓑ Ⓒ Ⓓ	96. Ⓐ Ⓑ Ⓒ Ⓓ
7. Ⓐ Ⓑ Ⓒ Ⓓ	37. Ⓐ Ⓑ Ⓒ Ⓓ	67. Ⓐ Ⓑ Ⓒ Ⓓ	97. Ⓐ Ⓑ Ⓒ Ⓓ
8. Ⓐ Ⓑ Ⓒ Ⓓ	38. Ⓐ Ⓑ Ⓒ Ⓓ	68. Ⓐ Ⓑ Ⓒ Ⓓ	98. Ⓐ Ⓑ Ⓒ Ⓓ
9. Ⓐ Ⓑ Ⓒ Ⓓ	39. Ⓐ Ⓑ Ⓒ Ⓓ	69. Ⓐ Ⓑ Ⓒ Ⓓ	99. Ⓐ Ⓑ Ⓒ Ⓓ
10. Ⓐ Ⓑ Ⓒ Ⓓ	40. Ⓐ Ⓑ Ⓒ Ⓓ	70. Ⓐ Ⓑ Ⓒ Ⓓ	100. Ⓐ Ⓑ Ⓒ Ⓓ
11. Ⓐ Ⓑ Ⓒ Ⓓ	41. Ⓐ Ⓑ Ⓒ Ⓓ	71. Ⓐ Ⓑ Ⓒ Ⓓ	
12. Ⓐ Ⓑ Ⓒ Ⓓ	42. Ⓐ Ⓑ Ⓒ Ⓓ	72. Ⓐ Ⓑ Ⓒ Ⓓ	
13. Ⓐ Ⓑ Ⓒ Ⓓ	43. Ⓐ Ⓑ Ⓒ Ⓓ	73. Ⓐ Ⓑ Ⓒ Ⓓ	
14. Ⓐ Ⓑ Ⓒ Ⓓ	44. Ⓐ Ⓑ Ⓒ Ⓓ	74. Ⓐ Ⓑ Ⓒ Ⓓ	
15. Ⓐ Ⓑ Ⓒ Ⓓ	45. Ⓐ Ⓑ Ⓒ Ⓓ	75. Ⓐ Ⓑ Ⓒ Ⓓ	
16. Ⓐ Ⓑ Ⓒ Ⓓ	46. Ⓐ Ⓑ Ⓒ Ⓓ	76. Ⓐ Ⓑ Ⓒ Ⓓ	
17 Ⓐ Ⓑ Ⓒ Ⓓ	47. Ⓐ Ⓑ Ⓒ Ⓓ	77. Ⓐ Ⓑ Ⓒ Ⓓ	
18. Ⓐ Ⓑ Ⓒ Ⓓ	48. Ⓐ Ⓑ Ⓒ Ⓓ	78. Ⓐ Ⓑ Ⓒ Ⓓ	
19. Ⓐ Ⓑ Ⓒ Ⓓ	49. Ⓐ Ⓑ Ⓒ Ⓓ	79. Ⓐ Ⓑ Ⓒ Ⓓ	
20. Ⓐ Ⓑ Ⓒ Ⓓ	50. Ⓐ Ⓑ Ⓒ Ⓓ	80. Ⓐ Ⓑ Ⓒ Ⓓ	
21. Ⓐ Ⓑ Ⓒ Ⓓ	51. Ⓐ Ⓑ Ⓒ Ⓓ	81. Ⓐ Ⓑ Ⓒ Ⓓ	
22. Ⓐ Ⓑ Ⓒ Ⓓ	52. Ⓐ Ⓑ Ⓒ Ⓓ	82. Ⓐ Ⓑ Ⓒ Ⓓ	
23. Ⓐ Ⓑ Ⓒ Ⓓ	53. Ⓐ Ⓑ Ⓒ Ⓓ	83. Ⓐ Ⓑ Ⓒ Ⓓ	
24. Ⓐ Ⓑ Ⓒ Ⓓ	54. Ⓐ Ⓑ Ⓒ Ⓓ	84. Ⓐ Ⓑ Ⓒ Ⓓ	
25. Ⓐ Ⓑ Ⓒ Ⓓ	55. Ⓐ Ⓑ Ⓒ Ⓓ	85. Ⓐ Ⓑ Ⓒ Ⓓ	
26. Ⓐ Ⓑ Ⓒ Ⓓ	56. Ⓐ Ⓑ Ⓒ Ⓓ	86. Ⓐ Ⓑ Ⓒ Ⓓ	
27. Ⓐ Ⓑ Ⓒ Ⓓ	57. Ⓐ Ⓑ Ⓒ Ⓓ	87. Ⓐ Ⓑ Ⓒ Ⓓ	
28. Ⓐ Ⓑ Ⓒ Ⓓ	58. Ⓐ Ⓑ Ⓒ Ⓓ	88. Ⓐ Ⓑ Ⓒ Ⓓ	
29. Ⓐ Ⓑ Ⓒ Ⓓ	59. Ⓐ Ⓑ Ⓒ Ⓓ	89. Ⓐ Ⓑ Ⓒ Ⓓ	
30. Ⓐ Ⓑ Ⓒ Ⓓ	60. Ⓐ Ⓑ Ⓒ Ⓓ	90. Ⓐ Ⓑ Ⓒ Ⓓ	

Practice Test 3

Name: _____   Date: _____

STATE PORTION

#						#				
1.	Ⓐ	Ⓑ	Ⓒ	Ⓓ		31.	Ⓐ	Ⓑ	Ⓒ	Ⓓ
2.	Ⓐ	Ⓑ	Ⓒ	Ⓓ		32.	Ⓐ	Ⓑ	Ⓒ	Ⓓ
3.	Ⓐ	Ⓑ	Ⓒ	Ⓓ		33.	Ⓐ	Ⓑ	Ⓒ	Ⓓ
4.	Ⓐ	Ⓑ	Ⓒ	Ⓓ		34.	Ⓐ	Ⓑ	Ⓒ	Ⓓ
5.	Ⓐ	Ⓑ	Ⓒ	Ⓓ		35.	Ⓐ	Ⓑ	Ⓒ	Ⓓ
6.	Ⓐ	Ⓑ	Ⓒ	Ⓓ		36.	Ⓐ	Ⓑ	Ⓒ	Ⓓ
7.	Ⓐ	Ⓑ	Ⓒ	Ⓓ		37.	Ⓐ	Ⓑ	Ⓒ	Ⓓ
8.	Ⓐ	Ⓑ	Ⓒ	Ⓓ		38.	Ⓐ	Ⓑ	Ⓒ	Ⓓ
9.	Ⓐ	Ⓑ	Ⓒ	Ⓓ		39.	Ⓐ	Ⓑ	Ⓒ	Ⓓ
10.	Ⓐ	Ⓑ	Ⓒ	Ⓓ		40.	Ⓐ	Ⓑ	Ⓒ	Ⓓ
11.	Ⓐ	Ⓑ	Ⓒ	Ⓓ						
12.	Ⓐ	Ⓑ	Ⓒ	Ⓓ						
13.	Ⓐ	Ⓑ	Ⓒ	Ⓓ						
14.	Ⓐ	Ⓑ	Ⓒ	Ⓓ						
15.	Ⓐ	Ⓑ	Ⓒ	Ⓓ						
16.	Ⓐ	Ⓑ	Ⓒ	Ⓓ						
17	Ⓐ	Ⓑ	Ⓒ	Ⓓ						
18.	Ⓐ	Ⓑ	Ⓒ	Ⓓ						
19.	Ⓐ	Ⓑ	Ⓒ	Ⓓ						
20.	Ⓐ	Ⓑ	Ⓒ	Ⓓ						
21.	Ⓐ	Ⓑ	Ⓒ	Ⓓ						
22.	Ⓐ	Ⓑ	Ⓒ	Ⓓ						
23.	Ⓐ	Ⓑ	Ⓒ	Ⓓ						
24.	Ⓐ	Ⓑ	Ⓒ	Ⓓ						
25.	Ⓐ	Ⓑ	Ⓒ	Ⓓ						
26.	Ⓐ	Ⓑ	Ⓒ	Ⓓ						
27.	Ⓐ	Ⓑ	Ⓒ	Ⓓ						
28.	Ⓐ	Ⓑ	Ⓒ	Ⓓ						
29.	Ⓐ	Ⓑ	Ⓒ	Ⓓ						
30.	Ⓐ	Ⓑ	Ⓒ	Ⓓ						

National Portion

1. What is the name given to the estimate amount on a mortgage?

    A. Pre-approval
    B. Post-approval
    C. Principal
    D. Mortgage

2. What is the actual amount of space a tenant can lay carpet and place furniture?

    A. Usable Square Footage
    B. Rentable square footage
    C. Common areas
    D. Service areas

3. What is the name given to an amount of money borrowed to facilitate the purchase of a property?

    A. Escrow
    B. Interest
    C. Down payment
    D. Principal

4. What type of mortgage loan is made available through the United States Department of Veterans Affairs?

    A. Blanket mortgage
    B. Balloon mortgage
    C. Graduated mortgage
    D. VA mortgage

5. What is the value obtained by deducting applied payments from original amortization?

    A. Full term
    B. Paid term
    C. Principal term
    D. Remaining term

6. What is the arrangement that allows a seller to lease a property from a purchaser after selling it?

    A. Leaseback
    B. Leasehold
    C. Sublease
    D. Proprietary lease

7. What type of easement attaches rights to a tenant instead of the land?

    A. Easement appurtenant
    B. Easement in gross
    C. Prescriptive easement
    D. All the above

8. What is the penalty charge for paying back a loan ahead of the scheduled payment plan?

    A. Defaulting penalty
    B. Interest
    C. Prepayment penalty
    D. Principal amount

9. What is an insurance premium paid by the buyer to the lender in order to protect the lender from default on a mortgage?

   A. Hazard insurance
   B. Homeowner's insurance
   C. Private mortgage insurance
   D. Title insurance

10. What is the name given to a party that acts in conjunction with a lender to originate a loan?

    A. Mortgage broker
    B. Third party originator
    C. Lender
    D. Intermediate

11. What is the term used to describe the alteration of a property in order to increase its market value?

    A. Capital Improvement
    B. Preventive maintenance
    C. Appreciation
    D. Common charges

12. What is the tax levied on transfer of property?

    A. Capital gains tax
    B. Deductible tax
    C. Property tax
    D. Transfer tax

13. Which of the following is an appraisal method in real estate?

    A. Sales Comparison Approach
    B. Cost Approach
    C. Income Approach
    D. All of the above

14. For at least how long must an asset be held before being sold to be categorized as long-term capital gains?

    A. One month
    B. Six months
    C. One year
    D. Two years

15. Which of these is considered an operating expense?

    A. Repairs
    B. Depreciation
    C. Payroll
    D. All of the above

16. What is an unlawful detainer?

    A. Forcing rent payments for tenants who have already moved out
    B. Refusing to leave a property despite expiration or termination of lease
    C. Listing a property whose lease has not expired
    D. Subletting a property without permission from the landlord

17. What is the freeze placed on a mortgage loan for a period of time?

    A. Cessation
    B. Amortization
    C. Rate lock
    D. Interest freeze

18. What type of lease gives the tenant an option to purchase the property?

    A. Leaseback
    B. Lease option
    C. Leasehold
    D. Gross lease

19. What is conditioner capacity?

    A. This is the capacity of an air conditioner to heat or cool the room
    B. The space used up by an air conditioner
    C. The strength of an air conditioner
    D. The cooling capacity of an air conditioner and is measured in tons

20. What is the name given to an individual that acts in intermediate for brokers and lenders?

    A. Mortgage broker
    B. Mortgage banker
    C. Attorney
    D. Intermediate

21. If a property is taxed at 30% with a tax levy of $105,000, what is its assessed value?

    A. $136,500
    B. $146,666
    C. $350,000
    D. None of the above

22. What is the notice given when a tenant has a pet in a complex that has no pets policy?

    A. Notice to cure
    B. Notice to quit
    C. Notice of default
    D. Notice of termination

23. What is a roof's vertical rise in inches divided by its horizontal span in feet?

    A. Depth
    B. Width
    C. Pitch
    D. Length

24. Who engages the services of a broker?

    A. The client
    B. The neighbor
    C. The contractor
    D. The appraiser

25. Right of way would be best defined as?

    A.   Escheat
    B.   Easement
    C.   Right of ingress
    D.   Encumbrance

26. Who can get partial exemptions from property taxes?

    A.   Disabled
    B.   Schools
    C.   Shelters
    D.   Markets

27. What age must a person be to get a Real Estate license?

    A.   16 years
    B.   18 years
    C.   30 years
    D.   43 years

28. Which electricity conductor plays the same role as a circuit board?

    A.   Cell
    B.   Capacitor
    C.   Fuse
    D.   Switch

29. What is the definition of a bilateral contract?

    A.   A contract that involves only the promisor
    B.   A contract that involves only the promisee
    C.   A contract that involves both a promisor and promisee
    D.   A contract that allows both parties to drop all claims and get out of the contract

30. What is real property tax based on?

    A.   Assessed value
    B.   CMA
    C.   Appraisal
    D.   Taxable value

31. What agency is responsible for protecting wetlands?

    A.   CERCLA
    B.   Environmental Protection Agency
    C.   FEMA
    D.   NY Health Department

32. What is a schedule of the projected future income and expenses for a real estate investment?

    A.   IOU
    B.   Invoice
    C.   Promissory note
    D.   Pro Forma Statement

33. What is an agent required to do if a client refuses to sign an agency disclosure form?

    A. Terminate relationship
    B. Create record of refusal in writing
    C. Continue without record of the refusal
    D. Take legal action against the client

34. What is a general voluntary lien?

    A. Mortgage
    B. Taxes
    C. Revenues
    D. Duties

35. If a salesperson's commission is not paid, he resorts to?

    A. Buyer
    B. Seller
    C. Broker
    D. Lender

36. What type of tenancy exists where property is owned by a single individual?

    A. Joint tenancy
    B. Ownership in severalty
    C. Tenancy in entirety
    D. Tenancy in common

37. Who are testers in real estate?

    A. People who pose as real estate clients to check if fair housing is being practiced
    B. People who assess the value of a property
    C. People who pose as borrowers to ensure proper loaning practices
    D. People who approach the seller without the intention of buying

38. What is the term used to describe the natural increase of land?

    A. Expansion
    B. Avulsion
    C. Erosion
    D. Accretion

39. What is the length of time allowed for depreciation for a residential property?

    A. 5 years
    B. 27.5 years
    C. 39 years
    D. 70 years

40. What is the term used to describe personal property?

    A. Chattel
    B. Investment
    C. Possession
    D. Real property

41. Which act was enacted to ensure parties involved in a real estate transaction receive complete settlement cost disclosure?

- A. RESPA
- B. FHA
- C. Clean Water Act
- D. Civil Rights Act

42. What is the name given to the downward movement of water through soil?

- A. Absorption
- B. Filtration
- C. Percolation
- D. Proration

43. What type of income is generated by investing in a limited partnership?

- A. Active income
- B. Passive income
- C. Surplus income
- D. Savings

44. What mortgage type allows the mortgagor to make payments only on the interest accrued?

- A. Blanket mortgage
- B. Balloon mortgage
- C. Graduated mortgage
- D. Straight term mortgage

45. Mary's agent helped her purchase a property and negotiated a mortgage for her. This agent also represented the seller. What type of agent did Mary engage?

- A. Single agent
- B. Dual agent
- C. Double agent
- D. None of the above

46. What is the land survey process that involves the surveyor starting at an easily identifiable point and describing the property in terms of courses and distances and eventually returning to the starting point?

- A. ALTA
- B. Boundary construction
- C. Metes and bounds
- D. Topographic surveys

47. What arrangement allows the seller to absorb an existing loan in order to allow the buyer another mortgage?

- A. Simple mortgage
- B. Wraparound mortgage
- C. Mortgage by conditional sale
- D. Reverse mortgage

48. Which real estate participants are legally required to be licensed?

- A. Sellers
- B. Buyers
- C. Lenders
- D. Real estate agents and brokers

49. What is the term used to refer to the act of mixing money belonging to a client with one's own funds?

   A. Commingling
   B. Investing
   C. Stealing
   D. Saving

50. What is the effect of a larger money supply on the interest rates?

   A. They decrease
   B. They increase
   C. Remains constant
   D. They have no relationship

51. What is a homeowner's policy that covers two parts: property and liability?

   A. HO1
   B. HO2
   C. HO3
   D. HO4

52. What is the name given to tax calculated based on the value of an asset?

   A. Ad valorem tax
   B. Property tax
   C. Capital gains tax
   D. Transfer tax

53. What kind of lease agreement requires the landlord to pay for all expenses?

   A. Gross lease
   B. Ground lease
   C. Net lease
   D. Sublease

54. If a seller nets $442,000 from the sale of her home, and the commission is 5%, how much did the home sell for?

   A. $464,100
   B. $420,952
   C. $459,680
   D. None of the above

55. What is the short-term loan that covers the interval between selling one property and buying another?

   A. Bridge Loan
   B. Cash flow
   C. Cash on cash return
   D. Mortgage

56. What are the set rules established for condominium or co-op tenants?

   A. House rules
   B. Investment agreement
   C. Regulations
   D. Policy

57. Who is responsible for the rent in a sublease?

- A. New tenant
- B. Lessee
- C. Lessor
- D. Roommate

58. What income type does a salary fall under?

- A. Active income
- B. Passive income
- C. Savings
- D. Investment

59. What is the name given to an estate that gives the holder temporary possession rights?

- A. Concurrent estates
- B. Estate for years
- C. Freehold estates
- D. Leasehold estate

60. What is a permit issued to a builder stating the property is fit for occupancy?

- A. Certificate of occupancy
- B. Contract of sale
- C. Landmark designation
- D. Receipt of sales deposit

61. What kind of mortgage pays off the principal?

- A. Amortized loan
- B. Fixed- rate loan
- C. Floating rate loan
- D. Mortgage

62. What is the income that is left after all operating costs are paid in a real estate investment?

- A. Investment
- B. Net operating income
- C. Profit
- D. Revenue

63. Which lease allows for changes in rent within the lease term?

- A. Graduated lease
- B. Lease break
- C. Sublease
- D. Value point

64. What is the married couple's capital gains tax exclusion on the sale of their primary home?

- A. $50,000
- B. $75,000
- C. $250,000
- D. $500,000

65. What should a licensee do with their pocket card?

A. Advertise it
B. Carry a physical copy or have a digital image on a device
C. File it
D. Use it to get clients

66. Besides the real estate agents, who is eligible for a license?

A. Attorney
B. Broker
C. Mortgage broker
D. Lender

67. What is a single person's capital gains tax exclusion?

A. $25,000
B. $100,000
C. $250,000
D. $500,000

68. What is the term given to violation of neighbor's property by trespassing?

A. Easement
B. Escheat
C. Encroachment
D. Encumbrance

69. What type of insurance is referred to as renters insurance?

A. HO1
B. HO2
C. HO3
D. HO4

70. What is a form of co-ownership by which all parties have undivided interests in the property but no right of survivorship?

A. Tenancy in common
B. Tenancy in entirety
C. Joint tenancy
D. Ownership in severalty

71. What conveys a grantor's interest in real property?

A. Deed
B. Insurance
C. Title
D. Warrant

72. What is the chain of deeds and other documents used in transferring title of land from one owner to another consecutively?

A. Abstract of title
B. Deed chain
C. History of deed
D. Chain of title

73. If you paid a down payment of $200,000 for a property worth $1,000,000 dollars and you currently rent it out for $4,000 a month, what is the cash-on-cash return?

    A.   4%
    B.   4.8%
    C.   20%
    D.   24%

74. What is a Certificate of Eligibility?

    A.   Certificate that shows one is to be exempt from property tax
    B.   Certificate that is presented by veterans to show proof that they have met the minimum service requirements to be eligible for a VA loan
    C.   Certificate that shows a construction is fit for occupancy
    D.   Certificate that shows merit

75. What is the insurance policy that protects a lender from loss due to disputes over ownership of a property and defects in the title?

    A.   Hazard insurance
    B.   Home warranty
    C.   Homeowner's insurance
    D.   Title insurance

76. Property that has a divided form of ownership is called?

    A.   Cooperative
    B.   Planned unit development
    C.   Time-share
    D.   Joint tenants

77. What is the definition of a syndication?

    A.   Income that is earned by a spouse prior to marriage
    B.   Land that is divided into smaller pieces of land
    C.   Mutual funds that invest in rental properties
    D.   Real estate that is purchased by a group which includes at least one sponsor and several investors

78. Which of the following is **not** an essential element of a contract?

    A.   Notarized signature
    B.   Consideration
    C.   Agreement by offer and acceptance
    D.   Competent parties

79. Which listing agreement allows the owner of the listed property to sell the property on their own and not have to pay commission to the listing broker?

    A.   Open listing
    B.   Option listing
    C.   Exclusive agency listing
    D.   Both A and C

80. What is the listing agreement that gives the broker the payment of commission no matter who sells the property?

    A.   Entirety
    B.   Exclusive-right-to-sell listing
    C.   Open listing
    D.   Net Listing

81. Which is an example of functional obsolescence?

    A. Four bedrooms and one bathroom in a private residence
    B. All bedrooms located on the 2nd floor and only one bathroom located on the 1st floor
    C. Walking through one bedroom to get to another bedroom
    D. All of the above

82. Which act was passed to protect consumers from being scammed when purchasing raw land?

    A. Interstate Land Sales Full Disclosure Act
    B. Federal Fair Housing Act
    C. Equal Credit Opportunity Act
    D. Federal Real Estate Law

83. Which statement is a listing agent required to reveal to a prospective buyer?

    A. The physical health of the previous owner
    B. Renovations made within the last 5 years
    C. Re-zoning of a property
    D. The number of members living in a home

84. Real estate taxes are based on the value of a home. A property owner can be taxed additionally to help pay for projects that benefit the neighborhood. What is this type of tax called?

    A. Property tax
    B. Special assessment tax
    C. Progressive tax
    D. Capital gains tax

85. Which anti-trust violation applies to real estate?

    A.   Monopolization
    B.   Price-fixing
    C.   Collusion
    D.   None of the above

86. A _____ transfers a title of real property without the owner's consent.

    A.   Involuntary alienation
    B.   Redlining
    C.   Lien
    D.   Deed restriction

87. Which of the following is a common-law fiduciary duty?

    A.   Care
    B.   Accounting
    C.   Confidentiality
    D.   All of the above

88. Which type of lease increases at specific intervals?

    A.   Lease option
    B.   Graduated lease
    C.   Month to month lease
    D.   Triple net lease

89. A _____ can be granted by a zoning board if a property owner demonstrates a need to deviate from the current zoning requirements.

    A. Variance
    B. Moratorium
    C. Quitclaim
    D. Encumbrance

90. A defect that is not apparent after an ordinary inspection is called a(n) _____.

    A. Undisclosed defect
    B. Material defect
    C. Arbitration
    D. Latent defect

91. Which of the following statement(s) is(are) true about an option to purchase agreement?

    A. The seller is required to accept any offer that meets all of their needs
    B. The buyer is required to buy the property once the option agreement has been completed
    C. The seller can change their mind about the offer if a better offer has been received
    D. All of the above

92. Which type of loan requires the debt ratio to not exceed 41%?

    A. Federal Housing Administration loan
    B. VA loan
    C. Interest-only mortgage
    D. Adjustable rate mortgage

93. What is the difference between a lien theory and a title theory?

    A. Lien theory is when the title is held by the lender until the final payment is made
    B. Title theory is when the title is held by the borrower
    C. Lien theory is when the title is held by the borrower with a lien to the property granted to the lender
    D. In title theory the borrower never holds the title

94. This type of loan is banned in 25 states and increases the principal balance of a loan because of a failure to make payments to the loan that covers the interest due?

    A. Conventional loan
    B. Negative amortization
    C. Unsecured loan
    D. Open-ended loan

95. Which of the following will terminate an agency in a broker-seller relationship?

    A. The owner declares bankruptcy
    B. The broker gets assistance from another broker to help sell the property
    C. The owner moves out of the property
    D. All of the above

96. Which type of community groups housing, recreation and commercial units into one self-contained development?

    A. Timeshare
    B. Mixed-use development
    C. Cooperative
    D. Planned unit development

97. A(an)_____ allows crops produced annually to be harvested from the owner or tenant who planted the crops even if the property was sold or the lease expired.

A. Lis pendens
B. Suit to partition
C. Emblement
D. Index lease

98. Which law requires lenders to disclose all loan costs to the borrower?

A. Borrower Transparency Act
B. Regulation Z
C. Fair Housing Act
D. Federal Trade Commission

99. This is the largest real estate organization in the United States.

A. National Association of Realtors
B. The Realtors Association
C. United States Realtors Association
D. None of the above

100. Which of the following factors affects real estate supply?

A. Labor force
B. Government controls
C. Construction costs
D. All of the above

THIS IS THE END OF THE NATIONAL PORTION.

State Portion

1. This type of zoning preserves free space and places homes close together.

   A. Spot zoning
   B. Cluster zoning
   C. Impact zoning
   D. Hybrid zoning

2. A _____ must sign the deed in order for it to be valid in the state of North Carolina.

   A. Buyer's agent
   B. Grantor
   C. Selling broker
   D. None of the above

3. Which of the following is a factor considered by the North Carolina courts when determining the legality of spot zoning?

   A. The size of the area
   B. The degree of compatibility
   C. The impact of rezoning on neighboring landowners
   D. All of the above

4. North Carolina defines a subdivision as all divisions of a tract or parcel of land into _____ or more lots, building sites or other divisions.

   A. 3
   B. 5
   C. 2
   D. 6

5. A developer must have streets approved, based on the construction standards set by the _____.

   A.   Federal Department of Transportation
   B.   North Carolina Department of Transportation
   C.   State House of Representatives
   D.   NCREC

6. North Carolina is a disclosure state, which means the seller must provide a completed _____ to the buyer prior to the contract to be signed.

   A.   Residential property disclosure statement
   B.   Appraisal of the property
   C.   Property statement
   D.   No form is required

7. Who certifies the local building inspectors?

   A.   NCREC
   B.   North Carolina Department of Insurance
   C.   Commission of inspectors
   D.   None of the above

8. A _____ is required to build a new structure or alter a repair on an existing building or property.

   A.   Building permit
   B.   License
   C.   Zoning permit
   D.   Inspection

9. A _____ is provided by the building inspector once a completed structure has been inspected and deemed satisfactory.

    A. Inspection completion document
    B. Certificate of satisfaction
    C. Inspection permit
    D. Certificate of occupancy

11. Which of the following could result in disciplinary action by the North Carolina Real Estate Commission?

    A. A broker failing to properly disclose material regarding road access
    B. A broker failing to sell a home at the listed price
    C. A broker failing the licensing exam
    D. All of the above could result in disciplinary action

10. A zone changing from commercial to residential is an example of _____.

    A. Downzoning
    B. Upzoning
    C. Taking
    D. Variance

12. A _____ imposes a restriction on the use of land to preserve the value and enjoyment of adjoining land.

    A. Permit
    B. Restrictive covenant
    C. Zoning laws
    D. Blockbusting

13. North Carolina is a(n) _____ state, in other words let the buyer beware.

    A. Arbitration
    B. Attorney
    C. Caveat emptor
    D. Tenancy by the entirety

14. In North Carolina, a broker in charge is the agent of the principal and the _____ of the principal are brokers employed by the firm.

    A. Sales agent
    B. Subagent
    C. Provisional broker
    D. None of the above

15. The _____, states that nothing has to be in writing or by oral agreement, it is illegal under North Carolina real estate law.

    A. Implied agency agreement
    B. Apparent agency agreement
    C. Express agency agreement
    D. None of the above

16. Which of the following statements is true regarding dual agency in the state of North Carolina?

    A. Dual agency is illegal in North Carolina
    B. All parties must be informed and must consent to the broker
    C. The buyer is the only person that must be informed and consent
    D. Consent is not required for dual agency

17. The North Carolina Homestead exemption is for residence who are 65 or older or totally and permanently disabled. The resident must also have a salary that does not exceed _____.

    A. $25,000
    B. $35,000
    C. $31,000
    D. $30,000

18. What does the homestead exemption protect a homeowner from?

    A. Protect the value of the homeowner's principal residence from creditors and property taxes.
    B. Protect the homeowner from eminent domain
    C. Protect the surviving spouse of a deceased homeowner
    D. A&C only

19. The homestead exemption provides an exclusion of the taxable value of the homeowner's residence of either _____.

    A. $25,000 or 50% whichever is greater
    B. $30,000 or 40% whichever is lesser
    C. $30,000 or 40% whichever is greater
    D. $25,000 or 50% whichever is lesser

20. Which type of zoning separates and screens residential areas from non-residential areas.

    A. Cluster zoning
    B. Buffer zoning
    C. Performance zoning
    D. Incentive zoning

21. An inground swimming pool is considered a(n) _____.

    A. Public property
    B. Appurtenance
    C. Owner's rights
    D. None of the above

22. This is a legal document that records covenants on public record.

    A. Covenants form
    B. Declaration of restrictions
    C. Covenants and restrictions form
    D. None of the above

23. When land is transferred conditionally it is called a _____.

    A. Defeasible estate
    B. Covenant estate
    C. Restrictive estate
    D. Simple estate

24. Which of the following statements is true about a fee simple and a fee simple absolute?

    A. A fee simple is an unconditional fee simple absolute
    B. A fee simple absolute is an unconditional fee simple
    C. A company that is owned by a corporation is a fee simple if it can be determined by the dissolution of the corporation
    D. B&C only

25. Which of the following is considered a fixture?

    A. Electrical writing
    B. A refrigerator
    C. Light bulbs
    D. Above ground pool

26. The right of a tenant to make use of a property's wood is called a(n) _____.

    A. Estover
    B. Blocklist
    C. Arbitration
    D. Encroachment

27. A deed restriction on a home is called a(n) _____.

    A. Easement
    B. Encroachment
    C. Appurtenance
    D. Encumbrance

28. Which of the following is not a bundle of rights of an owner of a freehold estate?

    A. Quiet enjoyment
    B. Disposal of property by sale
    C. Control of use within the law
    D. All of the above

29. The exercise of the power of eminent domain is called _____.

A. Arbitration
B. Blockbusting
C. Condemnation
D. Quick take

30. Concurrent ownership is when two or more people own property at the same time. This is also considered _____.

A. Condominium
B. Timeshare
C. Co-ownership
D. Multi-ownership

31. A licensee would like to get their license reinstated after it was surrendered due to disciplinary proceedings. What must the licensee do for reinstatement?

A. Nothing, once the surrender period is over the license will automatically be reinstated
B. The licensee must submit a new application for reinstatement
C. The licensee must provide reason for the commission to reinstate the license
D. None of the above

32. The right a land has to be supported, in its natural state, by adjoining land is called _____.

A. Lateral support
B. Bilateral support
C. Horizontal support
D. None of the above

33. A _____ is a non-freehold estate of limited duration.

   A. Homestead estate
   B. Concurrent estate
   C. Leasehold estate
   D. Possessory estate

34. A pending lawsuit is also called a _____.

   A. Lis pendens
   B. Appurtenance
   C. Litigation
   D. Blockbusting

35. A _____ is in an area below the surface of land.

   A. Leasehold estate
   B. Possessory estate
   C. Freehold estate
   D. Mineral lease

36. This legal proceeding divides property owned by co-owners so that each one holds a title.

   A. Joint ownership
   B. Partition
   C. Littoral rights
   D. Arbitration

37. A _____ is a method of acquiring an easement with continuous and uninterrupted use without permission.

    A. Appurtenance
    B. Prescription
    C. Commingling
    D. Party wall

38. What is police power?

    A. The government's right to take private property for the benefit of the public
    B. The government's right to take unclaimed property of a deceased person
    C. The government's right to regulate the use of real property for the benefit of the public
    D. A&C only

39. An elderly father gives his daughter the right to use the family's house for as long as he lives. The daughter has possession of the house through _____.

    A. Ascension
    B. Commingling
    C. Life estate
    D. Pur autre vie

40. A person is set to inherit property upon the termination of the estate of the former owner. This is called _____.

    A. Pur autre vie
    B. Remainderman
    C. Commingling
    D. Arbitration

THIS IS THE END OF THE STATE PORTION.

Answer Key – National Portion

#		#		#		#		#	
1.	A	21.	C	41.	A	61.	A	81.	D
2.	A	22.	A	42.	C	62.	B	82.	A
3.	D	23.	C	43.	B	63.	A	83.	C
4.	D	24.	A	44.	D	64.	D	84.	B
5.	D	25.	B	45.	B	65.	B	85.	B
6.	A	26.	A	46.	C	66.	A	86.	A
7.	B	27.	B	47.	B	67.	C	87.	D
8.	C	28.	C	48.	D	68.	C	88.	B
9.	C	29.	C	49.	A	69.	D	89.	A
10.	B	30.	A	50.	A	70.	A	90.	D
11.	A	31.	B	51.	C	71.	A	91.	B
12.	D	32.	D	52.	A	72.	D	92.	A
13.	D	33.	B	53.	A	73.	D	93.	C
14.	C	34.	A	54.	D	74.	B	94.	B
15.	D	35.	C	55.	A	75.	D	95.	A
16.	B	36.	B	56.	A	76.	C	96.	D
17.	C	37.	A	57.	B	77.	D	97.	C
18.	B	38.	D	58.	A	78.	A	98.	B
19.	D	39.	B	59.	D	79.	D	99.	A
20.	A	40.	A	60.	A	80.	B	100.	D

1. **A) Pre-approval**

Prior to purchasing a property, the borrower can visit a lender and obtain a pre-approval letter stating the amount of credit the lender is willing to accord the buyer which will help determine what the buyer can afford.

2. **A) Usable Square Footage**

Usable square footage is the amount of space you actually occupy in a leased space.

3. **D) Principal**

The principal is the amount of money that a lender gives a borrower to facilitate property purchase. Payment of principal results in increase in borrower's equity.

4.   **D) VA mortgage**

This is a mortgage plan that is tailored to assist service members and their surviving spouses to become homeowners. There are usually a lot of qualifying standards put in place to be eligible for this type of mortgage and it is usually offered by banks and other credit facilities. The Veteran administration usually acts as a guarantor for the loan. Qualified Veterans are usually eligible for 100% financing.

5.   **D) Remaining term**

It is usually used to complete the period of time left on a loan and the amount of principal payment to be covered within that period.

6.   **A) Leaseback**

This is an arrangement that allows a seller to lease a property from the purchaser on transfer of ownership. The details surrounding the lease arrangement are usually discussed immediately after the sale.

7.   **B) Easement in gross**

Easement in gross is the agreement that attaches rights to the tenant over the property. Transfer of the land results in an immediate termination of the agreement. The agreement can be renegotiated with the new tenant over time.

8.   **C) Prepayment penalty**

This is the penalty placed on the significant payment of a mortgage within the first five years of the loan. This penalty exists to protect lenders from loss of interest income.

9.   **C) Private mortgage insurance**

These insurance payments are usually discontinued once a buyer builds up to 20% equity on the home.

10.   **B) Third party originator**

This is any third party used to originate a loan. Lenders often employ the services of third-party moderators to underwrite and originate loans. They offer no ongoing and lasting responsibility for the mortgage.

11. **A) Capital Improvement**

This is the addition of a permanent change in a structure or restoration of damaged property. It is done to increase the longevity and market value of the property. For an item to be considered a capital investment, it has to be a permanent addition and capable of improving the value of the property.

12. **D) Transfer tax**

This is any tax that is levied on transfer of ownership or title of property from one individual to another. It is usually non-deductible. It is usually levied at the local or federal level depending on the type of property changing ownership.

13. **D) All of the above**

Sales Comparison Approach, Cost Approach, and Income Approach are all appraisal methods.

14. **C) One year**

An asset must be held for at least one year before selling in order for profits to be categorized as long-term capital gains.

15. **D) All of the above**

Operating expenses include any costs associated with the operation and maintenance of an income-producing property.

16. **B) Refusing to leave a property despite expiration or termination of lease**

Commonly compared to an eviction, which is the legal removal of an individual from a lease due to violation of the terms of the agreement.

17. **C) Rate lock**

This occurs when lenders lock in a rate because it is the lowest rate being offered at the time. It is not a legally binding agreement and borrowers are allowed to abandon the rates based on the rising and falling.

18. **B) Lease option**

A lease option is a lease agreement that gives the tenant a choice to purchase the property within or at the end of the lease. It gives the buyer flexibility to make a purchase on the property. Usually involves an upfront agreement between the tenant and the landlord.

19.   **D) The cooling capacity of an air conditioner and is measured in tons**

It is determined by measuring the size of the space being serviced by the air conditioner. The size area of the room is measured and multiplied by 25 BTU to determine the cooling capacity required in an air conditioner.

20.   **A) Mortgage broker**

This is an individual that serves as an intermediate between lenders and brokers. A mortgage broker facilitates negotiations of interest rates and takes circulation of paperwork between the lender and the borrowers.

21.   **C) $350,000**

$105,000 / 0.3 = $350,000

22.   **A) Notice to cure**

This is a notice given to a leaseholder by the landlord regarding participation in activities that are not allowed in the building. The tenant is given 10 days to correct the mistake. Refusal to make adjustment results in the tenant being served a notice of termination.

23.   **C) Pitch**

Defines the steepness of a roof. It is used to determine the material used for roofing and the space in the attic. It is also used to determine stability so that corrective measures can be undertaken early.

24.   **A) The client**

A broker is required to work in the best interests of the client to ensure the best possible deal for the client.

25.   **B) Easement**

This is the right to use another person's land temporarily without actually possessing it.

26.   **A) Disabled**

Disabled, veterans, elderly, farmers, Gold Star Parents, and Star Program Homeowners. The above classes of people can get partial tax exemption by having the values of their homes reduced translating in reduced property taxes.

27.   **B) 18 years**

This is the minimum required age for a real estate agent that has taken the education course and passed the qualifying exam.

28.   C) Fuse

A fuse is a small conductor that is designed to melt under high current to break the circuit. A fuse should always maintain a series connection to the component of the circuit.

29.   C) A contract that involves both a promisor and promisee

This contract occurs when both parties exchange a promise for a promise. Both parties enter into an agreement to fulfill their side of the bargain. Each party is also an obligor and obligee in this type of contract.

30.   A) Assessed value

Assessed value is the monetary value assigned to a property and is usually used to determine the value of a property for the purpose of taxation.

31.   B) Environmental Protection Agency

The Environmental Protection Agency is tasked with protecting both human and environmental health. The agency creates standards and laws promoting health of individuals and the environment and participates in upholding them by administering correcting efforts like CERCLA.

32.   D) Pro Forma Statement

This is an estimate summary of income production if the current trends are maintained. This is usually in multifamily properties in order to help the investor understand general financial operations of the property.

33.   B) Create record of refusal in writing

In the case where a client refuses to sign a disclosure, the agent is required to clearly state the names of the client and the facts surrounding the refusal to sign the disclosure. An agent is also required to sign a declaration in the presence of a notary public and have it notarized.

34.   A) Mortgage

A voluntary lien is a claim a debtor has over the property of another and is initiated by the debtor as in the case of a mortgage. The debtor cannot legally sell the property as it is considered collateral.

35.   **C) Broker**

An agent resorts to a broker for commission as the law does not allow salespersons to work independently and therefore cannot be paid directly. A broker on receiving commission from the sale of the property is required to split the commission amongst the agents that were involved in the transaction.

36.   **B) Ownership in severalty**

This is a situation where real estate is owned by a single person or entity providing the owner with the most control of the land. A sole owner is at will to take any action on the land such as selling or leasing.

37.   **A) People who pose as real estate clients to check if fair housing is being practiced**

Testing was initiated under the Fair Housing Act to ensure that housing providers act in accordance with the fair housing laws that protect against discrimination based on race, origin and gender.

38.   **D) Accretion**

This is the natural growth of a parcel of land due to mother nature. It occurs due to accumulation of soil on the shoreline of a water body. A decrease due to erosion is also possible.

39.   **B) 27.5 years**

Depreciation is the loss of value of a property due to age, wear and tear. A residential property can only declare depreciation after 27.5 years in order to reduce the value of the property and property tax on the property.

40.   **A) Chattel**

A chattel is a tangible property which is either mobile or immobile. However, this term cannot be used to describe real estate holdings.

41.   **A) RESPA**

The Real Estate Settling Procedures Act was developed in order to protect the parties involved in a real estate transaction from abuse during the settlement process. The act mandates lenders and brokers to disclose all matters crucial to the transaction service, settlement service and consumer protection laws

42. **C) Percolation**

This is the process in which water reaches the subsoil and roots. The pore space present in soil acts as a medium for the water to percolate. The ability of water to move through soil is dependent on the soil texture and structure. Some soils allow water to move very deep into the ground which may result in mixing with underground water reservoirs.

43. **B) Passive income**

This is income that is generated with minimal activity. It requires little to no effort to earn on a daily basis.

44. **D) Straight term mortgage**

A straight term mortgage is a mortgage that allows the mortgagor to make monthly payments on the interest accrued throughout the mortgage's lifespan. The principal remains unpaid until a set date where it becomes due for payment in full.

45. **B) Dual agent**

Mary's agent was able to perform the above transactions for her because he was working for both the Mary and the seller of the property.

46. **C) Metes and bounds**

This is a legal principle of land description and uses natural and artificial landmarks as boundaries. It is often used to describe irregular tracts of land. Metes defines straight line distances while bounds defines a less regular but identifiable lines. Measurements from an original point that is a monument and metes and bounds are described taking into account the boundaries. The process is repeated until the surveyor returns to the original point.

47. **B) Wraparound mortgage**

Wraparound mortgages are used to refinance property. They are mini loans that include the balance of the preexisting mortgage and an additional loan to cover the new property. The seller is granted a promissory note highlighting the amount due.

48. **D) Real estate agents and brokers**

They need to be licensed as they legally represent clients, buyers and sellers, in transferring ownership of property.

49. **A) Commingling**

This is a breach of trust that occurs when a representative of a client mixes individual funds with that of the client making it impossible to determine the amounts that belong to each individual.

50.   **A) They decrease**

Money supply is influenced by supply and demand. An increase in the money supply will result in a decreased interest rate making it easier to borrow and vice versa. Therefore, money and interest rates have an inversely proportional relationship.

51.   **C) HO3**

A home owner's policy is a property insurance that covers losses and damages done to the insured's house and assets within the home. It also provides liability coverage against accidents within the home.

52.   **A) Ad valorem tax**

This is the tax levied by a municipality or local government entity based on assessed value. A public assessor is engaged to value the property in order to calculate the tax owed.

53.   **A) Gross lease**

This is a flat rent fee that included all expenses associated with ownership. It is inclusive of incidental charges such as taxes, insurance and utilities. It is an uncommon lease as landlords are unaware of the utility charges that may be incurred by a tenant.

54.   **D) None of the above**

$442,000 / (1 - 0.05) = $465,263

55.   **A) Bridge Loan**

This is a short-term loan of up to one year that provides cash flow enabling an individual to meet current obligations while awaiting permanent financing. It is often used in real estate to purchase a new home while awaiting the sale of the old property.

56.   **A) House rules**

These are set rules that have been put in place to ensure the comfort of the tenants living within the building. Violation of the house rules clause may result in eviction.

57.   **B) Lessee**

The original tenant for rent as he/she is liable to the owner. In case of overdue rent by the new tenant, the original tenant is held accountable.

58.   **A) Active income**

This is an income earned from performing services. Active participation is required to yield payment.

59. **D) Leasehold estate**

This is a lease that allows the tenant to have real property for an extended period of time. A time frame is agreed upon in the lease and the tenant is allowed to erect structures and profit from the business that has been established at the site.

60. **A) Certificate of occupancy**

This is a legal statement issued by the building department clearing a building for occupancy on meeting the building codes and other laws that surround the construction of a residential or commercial building. It can be obtained when a new building is constructed or an old building is repurposed.

61. **A) Amortized loan**

An amortized loan is a loan with a scheduled payment over a period of time that pays off the interest and principal. An amortized loan payment schedule focuses on paying off the interest and progresses into the principal.

62. **B) Net operating income**

This is a method used to value the income generating properties. To obtain the value, all expenses incurred during operations is subtracted to the total income produced by the property. To get the true value produced by the property, revenues earned must be included.

63. **A) Graduated lease**

A graduated lease is an agreement between the landlord and tenant that allows for periodic adjustment of monthly payments based on the market value of the property. It stands to benefit the landlord over a long period of time.

64. **D) $500,000**

In accordance with the Taxpayers Relief Act, a married couple is eligible for exclusion from capital gain tax for profits of up to $500,000. This is provided the property sold is a primary residence, they have been living in it for at least 2 years.

65. **B) Carry a physical copy or have a digital image on a device**

A pocket card is a pocket-sized license identifying the holder as a licensed agent. It contains a photo, name and business address of the holder.

66. **A) Attorney**

This is licensed broker that engages the services of other agents with intentions of splitting commission paid on the sale of a property.

67. **C) $250,000**

According to the Taxpayers relief act, a single person is eligible for a capital gains tax exemption for profits of up to $250,000 on the sale of a primary home.

68. **C) Encroachment**

Encroachment is a violation of property rights that occurs when an individual chooses to ignore set boundaries. This can be by extending structure into the neighbor's land or illegally entering the neighbor's property.

69. **D) HO4**

This insurance is designed to protect the insured and belongings from the covered losses. It covers liability, personal property, additional living expenses and medical payments to others. The insurance covers against risks specified in the policy.

70. **A) Tenancy in common**

A tenancy in common is a legal agreement where two or more people with undivided rights own a property. Members of a tenancy in common are not mandated to have equal rights and can enter the agreement at any time. Members of a tenancy in common are free to leave their shares to a beneficiary.

71. **A) Deed**

This is a signed legal document that conveys interest of a property and is used in cases of transfer of property provided a set of conditions are met. For a deed to hold legal merit, it must be filed in a public record.

72. **D) Chain of title**

This is an official ownership record of a property. It is usually maintained from a centralized registry. It is used widely to protect lenders and buyers from losses occurring due to errors in the title report.

73. **D) 24%**

($4,000 * 12) / $200,000 = 0.24

74. **B) Certificate that is presented by veterans to show proof that they have met the minimum service requirements to be eligible for a VA loan**

The Certificate of Eligibility serves as proof of a veteran's military service and must be provided to lenders during the VA loan process

75. **D) Title insurance**

A title insurance is based on the indemnity clause. It is taken by a buyer to protect the lender from loss caused by unidentified defects in the title. It acts against traditional insurance by protecting clients against claims on a past occurrence

76. **C) Time-share**

Also called vacation ownership, a time-share is shared ownership of a property. This type of property is typically a vacation property i.e. a condominium in a resort area. The buyer typically purchases a certain period of time for the unit, typically one- to two-week periods.

77. **D) Real estate that is purchased by a group which includes at least one sponsor and several investors**

Syndication is a method investors can use to invest in properties. Investors pool their financial and intellectual resources together to invest in properties that they would not be able to invest in individually.

78. **A) Notarized signature**

A notarized signature is not necessary in a contract. A legal purpose, competent parties, offer and acceptance, consideration and consent are the essential elements of a contract.

79. **D) Both A and C**

Exclusive agency listing is an agreement between a real estate firm and seller which grants the firm the exclusive rights to sell the property but also allows the seller to sell the home without paying a commission to the listing agent. An open listing is a property listing using multiple real estate agents. This type of listing also allows an owner to list and sell the property without paying a commission to an agent.

80. **B) Exclusive-right-to-sell listing**

A legal agreement under which the seller agrees to pay a commission to the listing broker. The listing broker acts as the agent and is provided commission whether the property is sold through the listing broker, seller or anyone else. An exception occurs when the seller names one or more individuals/entities as exemptions in the listing agreement.

81. **D) All of the above**

Functional obsolescence occurs when an objects usefulness or desirability has been reduced because of an outdated design feature. They are features that cannot be easily fixed.

82.   **A) Interstate Land Sales Full Disclosure Act**

Passed in 1968, this act protects against land scams by facilitating the regulation of interstate land sales. Developers need to register subdivisions that contain more than 100 or more nonexempt lots. They may also provide purchasers with a disclosure statement (property report) prior to a sale.

83.   **C) Re-zoning of a property**

A seller is required to disclose all known material facts regarding the property to a buyer. Personal information about the family is not required but a re-zoning of the property must be disclosed.

84.   **B) Special assessment tax**

Property owners are sometimes taxed for improvements that effect some of the property owners within a taxing district. Only the property owners who have been affected will be taxed. These taxes pay for local infrastructure projects such as sewer lines, or construction and maintenance of roads.

85.   **B) Price-fixing**

Price-fixing, boycotting and allocation of customer or markets are the most common anti-trust violations in real estate.

86.   **A) Involuntary alienation**

This type of alienation results from a levy and sale for taxes that are due from the owner. It can also result from bankruptcy or an insolvency.

87.   **D) All of the above**

A fiduciary duty is an obligation to act in the best interest of the principal. There are 6 common law duties care, obedience, loyalty, disclosure, accounting and confidentiality.

88.   **B) Graduated lease**

This type of lease allows the landlord to a periodic adjustment of monthly payments. An increase in monthly payments could be due to market conditions or because of increase in the value of leased property.

89.   **A) Variance**

A variance is a request to deviate from current zoning requirements. It allows the owner to use a piece of land in a way that it is not usually permitted by the zoning ordinance. It is a waiver and does not change the zoning law.

90. **D) Latent defect**

A latent defect is a fault in a property that cannot be found through a reasonable inspection prior to a sale. These hazards may jeopardize the structural integrity or the occupant's safety.

91. **B) The buyer is required to buy the property once the option agreement has been completed**

In an option to buy agreement the buyer needs to purchase the property if the optionee agrees to the contract. The optionee is not required accept the buyers offer.

92. **A) Federal Housing Administration loan**

The FHA loan is designed for low to moderate borrowers and require a lower minimum down payments and credit score than other conventional loans. This type of loan is issued by an approved lender and insured by the FHA.

93. **C) Lien theory is when the title is held by the borrower with a lien to the property granted to the lender**

The difference between lien theory and title theory is that in lien theory the buyer holds the deed while in title theory the lender holds the title until the final payment is made.

94. **B) Negative amortization**

Negative amortization is banned in 25 states and is considered predatory by the federal government. It refers to increasing the principal balance of a loan due to the failure to cover the interest that is due on that loan.

95. **A) The owner declares bankruptcy**

When a property owner declares bankruptcy the agency agreement is terminated. If the principal passes, then the agreement is also terminated. Getting help from other brokers and moving out of the property are not means for termination.

96. **D) Planned unit development**

The planned unit development is a type of development that has varied, and compatible land uses i.e. housing, recreations and commercial centers.

97. **C) Emblements**

Emblements are considered personal property. It allows whoever planted the crops the ability to harvest them no matter who owns the property.

98.   **B) Regulation Z**

This law gives the borrowers the right to cancel certain credit transactions. This law is also called the Truth-in-Lending Laws.

99.   **A) National Association of Realtors**

The NAR is an organization of real estate brokers that was created to promote the profession and foster professional behavior to its members. It has its own code of ethics that all members are required to adhere to.

100.   **D) All of the above**

All of the above factors affect the supply of real estate. The government financial policies will also affect the supply of real estate.

Answer Key – State Portion

1.	B	21.	B
2.	B	22.	B
3.	D	23.	A
4.	C	24.	B
5.	B	25.	A
6.	A	26.	A
7.	B	27.	D
8.	A	28.	D
9.	D	29.	C
10.	A	30.	C
11.	A	31.	B
12.	B	32.	A
13.	C	33.	C
14.	B	34.	A
15.	A	35.	D
16.	B	36.	B
17.	B	37.	B
18.	D	38.	C
19.	A	39.	D
20.	B	40.	B

1. **B) Cluster zoning**

In this type of zoning, density is determined for an entire area instead of on a lot-by-lot basis. The developer has greater flexibility in designing and placing structures.

2. **B) Grantor**

North Carolina requires a deed to be designed by a grantor for it to be considered valid.

3. **D) All of the above**

All of the above is considered. The degree of difference between the zoning of the surrounding area and the new zoning for the tracts in question is also considered.

4. **C) 2**

A subdivision is also considered for building sites or other types of divisions and includes all division of land involving the dedication of a new street or a change in existing streets.

5. **B) North Carolina Department of Transportation**

   This department is responsible for all modes of transportation in the state. This includes highways, rail, aviation, ferries, public transit, and bicycle lanes.

6. **A) Residential property disclosure statement**

   This form is required to be completed by the seller to the buyer. This form is required by the Residential property disclosure act.

7. **B) North Carolina Department of Insurance**

   The dept of insurance certifies the building inspectors who enforce the minimum construction standards.

8. **A) Building permit**

   A building permit is required and can be issued by a city clerk or another official prior to the start of building a new structure.

9. **D) Certificate of occupancy**

   This document shows that the building is safe to be occupied. This certificate is needed for new construction and changes in the use or occupancy of the building.

10. **A) Downzoning**

    When downzoning the zoning permit changes to a less intensive development than is currently permitted. In North Carolina, the state is not typically responsible for compensating property owners for resulting loss of value.

11. **A) A broker failing to properly disclose material regarding road access**

    Material facts about road access is knowledge that needs to be told to the buyer prior to the contract

12. **B) Restrictive covenant**

    A standard offer to purchase and contract cautions purchasers to review the restrictive covenants and any governing documents for the subdivision or any established owner's association.

13. **C) Caveat emptor**

    This principle states that the buyer alone is responsible for checking the quality and suitability of goods prior to the purchase.

14.   **B) Subagent**

The subagent of the principal are the brokers that are employed by the broker in charge. They are also considered the broker who brings in the buyer to purchase the property but has not listed it.

15.   **A) Implied agency agreement**

An implied agency agreement does not need to be in writing or verbally. North Carolina real estate law requires that all agency agreements to be in writing.

16.   **B) All parties must be informed and must consent to the broker**

Dual agency is legal in North Carolina both parties are informed and both parties consent otherwise it is illegal.

17.   **B) $31,000**

The homestead act is for residents of the state who are 65 or older, totally, and permanently disabled and have an income that does not exceed $31,000.

18.   **D) A&C only**

The homestead exemption is an exemption that allows a homeowner to protect the value of their principal residence from creditors or property taxes. It also protects surviving spouse of a deceased homeowner.

19.   **A) $25,000 or 50% whichever is greater**

The homeowner exemption allows for qualified homeowners to allow a portion of their appraised value to be excluded from property taxes.

20.   **B) Buffer zoning**

This zoning technique creates neutral space between two different types of buildings or properties with an interest in minimizing disturbances between potentially incompatible land uses.

21.   **B) Appurtenance**

Appurtenance are rights or privileges that come with owning a specific home. The rights or privileges move with the title.

22.   **B) Declaration of restrictions**

This document is recorded with the county recorder's office and is made a part of the office real estate records that runs with the land.

23.   **A) Defeasible estate**

If the condition is not met or if the condition is violated, then the estate transfer may be void or subject to annulment.

24.   **B) A fee simple absolute is an unconditional fee simple**

While a fee simple absolute is unconditional with no limits on the owner's rights in respect of the land, the fee simple is subject to a legal or equitable right of re-entry.

25.   **A) Electrical wiring**

Electrical wiring and plumbing are considered fixtures. A fixture is something that is permanently attached to the land.

26.   **A) Estover**

Estovers give tenants or a lessee the right to cut timber on the property for fuel or in making repairs.

27.   **D) Encumbrance**

This is a lien, claim or charge that is attached to and binding upon real property. This can be a claim against limitation on or liability against real estate.

28.   **D) All of the above**

All of the listed are considered bundle of rights of the owner of a freehold estate. Another right is the right to dispose of property through will or as a gift.

29.   **C) Condemnation**

This is the taking of private property, by the government, for public use, by paying compensation.

30.   **C) Co-ownership**

This type of real property is held by two or more persons at the same time. There are many types of co-ownerships such as tenancy in common and tenancy by the entirety.

31.   **B) The licensee must submit a new application for reinstatement**

In order for the licensee to get their license back after it has been surrendered due to disciplinary proceedings, the licensee is required to submit a new application for reinstatement.

32. **A) Lateral support**

This exists when the adjoining lands are side-by-side. Lateral support is the right of land to be naturally upheld by neighboring land and supported against subsidence.

33. **C) Leasehold estate**

This type of estate gives the tenant the right to live in a specified piece of property for a specified period of time.

34. **A) Lis pendens**

This is also called a pending lawsuit. The notice of pending litigation whose outcome may affect the title to all, or part of a new owner's property is called a lis pendens.

35. **D) Mineral lease**

This lease allows an individual the right to extract minerals such as iron, copper, and oil from a piece of property.

36. **B) Partition**

A conveyance or a contract divides land. This typically occurs when the owners cannot agree on whether they should sell.

37. **B) Prescription**

This is a type of easement that allows a person the right to use the property. To gain the easement it is necessary for the for the land to have been used openly, continuously, exclusively, and under claim of right for the appropriate statutory period.

38. **C) The government's right to regulate the use of real property for the benefit of the public**

Police power Is the state's right to regulate an individual's conduct or property to protect the health, safety, welfare and moral of the community.

39. **D) Pur Autre Vie**

This means for another's life. It is used to describe the duration of a property interest. It is a life estate measured by someone other than the life tenant.

40.   **B) Remainderman**

A remainderman holds an interest in the remainder and will become its possessor at a future time. It refers to a person who inherits or is entitled to inherit property upon the termination of the estate of the former owner.

Practice Test 4

Directions:

1.   You have a 4-hour time limit to complete the whole exam.

2.   To pass, you must answer at least 71 out of 100 questions correctly on the national portion **AND** at least 29 out of 40 questions on the state portion.

3.   Some questions will require mathematics. You may use a calculator.

4.   **Phones and pagers are not allowed. Having either will result in automatic dismissal from the exam and nullification of exam scores.**

Tips:

- Answer all questions even if you are unsure.
- Mark any questions you are stuck on and revisit them after you are done. The exam is timed so make sure you finish as many questions as you can.
- After reading the question, try answering it in your head first to avoid getting confused by the choices.
- Read the entire question before looking at the answers.
- Use the process of elimination to filter out choices that don't seem correct to increase your chances of selecting the correct answer.
- Be aware of important keywords like **not, sometimes, always,** and **never**. These words completely alter the ask of the question so it's important to keep track of them.

PLEASE READ THESE INSTRUCTIONS CAREFULLY.

Practice Test 4

Name: _____   Date: _____

NATIONAL PORTION

1. Ⓐ Ⓑ Ⓒ Ⓓ	31. Ⓐ Ⓑ Ⓒ Ⓓ	61. Ⓐ Ⓑ Ⓒ Ⓓ	91. Ⓐ Ⓑ Ⓒ Ⓓ
2. Ⓐ Ⓑ Ⓒ Ⓓ	32. Ⓐ Ⓑ Ⓒ Ⓓ	62. Ⓐ Ⓑ Ⓒ Ⓓ	92. Ⓐ Ⓑ Ⓒ Ⓓ
3. Ⓐ Ⓑ Ⓒ Ⓓ	33. Ⓐ Ⓑ Ⓒ Ⓓ	63. Ⓐ Ⓑ Ⓒ Ⓓ	93. Ⓐ Ⓑ Ⓒ Ⓓ
4. Ⓐ Ⓑ Ⓒ Ⓓ	34. Ⓐ Ⓑ Ⓒ Ⓓ	64. Ⓐ Ⓑ Ⓒ Ⓓ	94. Ⓐ Ⓑ Ⓒ Ⓓ
5. Ⓐ Ⓑ Ⓒ Ⓓ	35. Ⓐ Ⓑ Ⓒ Ⓓ	65. Ⓐ Ⓑ Ⓒ Ⓓ	95. Ⓐ Ⓑ Ⓒ Ⓓ
6. Ⓐ Ⓑ Ⓒ Ⓓ	36. Ⓐ Ⓑ Ⓒ Ⓓ	66. Ⓐ Ⓑ Ⓒ Ⓓ	96. Ⓐ Ⓑ Ⓒ Ⓓ
7. Ⓐ Ⓑ Ⓒ Ⓓ	37. Ⓐ Ⓑ Ⓒ Ⓓ	67. Ⓐ Ⓑ Ⓒ Ⓓ	97. Ⓐ Ⓑ Ⓒ Ⓓ
8. Ⓐ Ⓑ Ⓒ Ⓓ	38. Ⓐ Ⓑ Ⓒ Ⓓ	68. Ⓐ Ⓑ Ⓒ Ⓓ	98. Ⓐ Ⓑ Ⓒ Ⓓ
9. Ⓐ Ⓑ Ⓒ Ⓓ	39. Ⓐ Ⓑ Ⓒ Ⓓ	69. Ⓐ Ⓑ Ⓒ Ⓓ	99. Ⓐ Ⓑ Ⓒ Ⓓ
10. Ⓐ Ⓑ Ⓒ Ⓓ	40. Ⓐ Ⓑ Ⓒ Ⓓ	70. Ⓐ Ⓑ Ⓒ Ⓓ	100. Ⓐ Ⓑ Ⓒ Ⓓ
11. Ⓐ Ⓑ Ⓒ Ⓓ	41. Ⓐ Ⓑ Ⓒ Ⓓ	71. Ⓐ Ⓑ Ⓒ Ⓓ	
12. Ⓐ Ⓑ Ⓒ Ⓓ	42. Ⓐ Ⓑ Ⓒ Ⓓ	72. Ⓐ Ⓑ Ⓒ Ⓓ	
13. Ⓐ Ⓑ Ⓒ Ⓓ	43. Ⓐ Ⓑ Ⓒ Ⓓ	73. Ⓐ Ⓑ Ⓒ Ⓓ	
14. Ⓐ Ⓑ Ⓒ Ⓓ	44. Ⓐ Ⓑ Ⓒ Ⓓ	74. Ⓐ Ⓑ Ⓒ Ⓓ	
15. Ⓐ Ⓑ Ⓒ Ⓓ	45. Ⓐ Ⓑ Ⓒ Ⓓ	75. Ⓐ Ⓑ Ⓒ Ⓓ	
16. Ⓐ Ⓑ Ⓒ Ⓓ	46. Ⓐ Ⓑ Ⓒ Ⓓ	76. Ⓐ Ⓑ Ⓒ Ⓓ	
17. Ⓐ Ⓑ Ⓒ Ⓓ	47. Ⓐ Ⓑ Ⓒ Ⓓ	77. Ⓐ Ⓑ Ⓒ Ⓓ	
18. Ⓐ Ⓑ Ⓒ Ⓓ	48. Ⓐ Ⓑ Ⓒ Ⓓ	78. Ⓐ Ⓑ Ⓒ Ⓓ	
19. Ⓐ Ⓑ Ⓒ Ⓓ	49. Ⓐ Ⓑ Ⓒ Ⓓ	79. Ⓐ Ⓑ Ⓒ Ⓓ	
20. Ⓐ Ⓑ Ⓒ Ⓓ	50. Ⓐ Ⓑ Ⓒ Ⓓ	80. Ⓐ Ⓑ Ⓒ Ⓓ	
21. Ⓐ Ⓑ Ⓒ Ⓓ	51. Ⓐ Ⓑ Ⓒ Ⓓ	81. Ⓐ Ⓑ Ⓒ Ⓓ	
22. Ⓐ Ⓑ Ⓒ Ⓓ	52. Ⓐ Ⓑ Ⓒ Ⓓ	82. Ⓐ Ⓑ Ⓒ Ⓓ	
23. Ⓐ Ⓑ Ⓒ Ⓓ	53. Ⓐ Ⓑ Ⓒ Ⓓ	83. Ⓐ Ⓑ Ⓒ Ⓓ	
24. Ⓐ Ⓑ Ⓒ Ⓓ	54. Ⓐ Ⓑ Ⓒ Ⓓ	84. Ⓐ Ⓑ Ⓒ Ⓓ	
25. Ⓐ Ⓑ Ⓒ Ⓓ	55. Ⓐ Ⓑ Ⓒ Ⓓ	85. Ⓐ Ⓑ Ⓒ Ⓓ	
26. Ⓐ Ⓑ Ⓒ Ⓓ	56. Ⓐ Ⓑ Ⓒ Ⓓ	86. Ⓐ Ⓑ Ⓒ Ⓓ	
27. Ⓐ Ⓑ Ⓒ Ⓓ	57. Ⓐ Ⓑ Ⓒ Ⓓ	87. Ⓐ Ⓑ Ⓒ Ⓓ	
28. Ⓐ Ⓑ Ⓒ Ⓓ	58. Ⓐ Ⓑ Ⓒ Ⓓ	88. Ⓐ Ⓑ Ⓒ Ⓓ	
29. Ⓐ Ⓑ Ⓒ Ⓓ	59. Ⓐ Ⓑ Ⓒ Ⓓ	89. Ⓐ Ⓑ Ⓒ Ⓓ	
30. Ⓐ Ⓑ Ⓒ Ⓓ	60. Ⓐ Ⓑ Ⓒ Ⓓ	90. Ⓐ Ⓑ Ⓒ Ⓓ	

Practice Test 4

Name: _____   Date: _____

STATE PORTION

1.	Ⓐ Ⓑ Ⓒ Ⓓ	31. Ⓐ Ⓑ Ⓒ Ⓓ
2.	Ⓐ Ⓑ Ⓒ Ⓓ	32. Ⓐ Ⓑ Ⓒ Ⓓ
3.	Ⓐ Ⓑ Ⓒ Ⓓ	33. Ⓐ Ⓑ Ⓒ Ⓓ
4.	Ⓐ Ⓑ Ⓒ Ⓓ	34. Ⓐ Ⓑ Ⓒ Ⓓ
5.	Ⓐ Ⓑ Ⓒ Ⓓ	35. Ⓐ Ⓑ Ⓒ Ⓓ
6.	Ⓐ Ⓑ Ⓒ Ⓓ	36. Ⓐ Ⓑ Ⓒ Ⓓ
7.	Ⓐ Ⓑ Ⓒ Ⓓ	37. Ⓐ Ⓑ Ⓒ Ⓓ
8.	Ⓐ Ⓑ Ⓒ Ⓓ	38. Ⓐ Ⓑ Ⓒ Ⓓ
9.	Ⓐ Ⓑ Ⓒ Ⓓ	39. Ⓐ Ⓑ Ⓒ Ⓓ
10.	Ⓐ Ⓑ Ⓒ Ⓓ	40. Ⓐ Ⓑ Ⓒ Ⓓ
11.	Ⓐ Ⓑ Ⓒ Ⓓ	
12.	Ⓐ Ⓑ Ⓒ Ⓓ	
13.	Ⓐ Ⓑ Ⓒ Ⓓ	
14.	Ⓐ Ⓑ Ⓒ Ⓓ	
15.	Ⓐ Ⓑ Ⓒ Ⓓ	
16.	Ⓐ Ⓑ Ⓒ Ⓓ	
17	Ⓐ Ⓑ Ⓒ Ⓓ	
18.	Ⓐ Ⓑ Ⓒ Ⓓ	
19.	Ⓐ Ⓑ Ⓒ Ⓓ	
20.	Ⓐ Ⓑ Ⓒ Ⓓ	
21.	Ⓐ Ⓑ Ⓒ Ⓓ	
22.	Ⓐ Ⓑ Ⓒ Ⓓ	
23.	Ⓐ Ⓑ Ⓒ Ⓓ	
24.	Ⓐ Ⓑ Ⓒ Ⓓ	
25.	Ⓐ Ⓑ Ⓒ Ⓓ	
26.	Ⓐ Ⓑ Ⓒ Ⓓ	
27.	Ⓐ Ⓑ Ⓒ Ⓓ	
28.	Ⓐ Ⓑ Ⓒ Ⓓ	
29.	Ⓐ Ⓑ Ⓒ Ⓓ	
30.	Ⓐ Ⓑ Ⓒ Ⓓ	

National Portion

1. Which of the following is considered commercial real estate?

   A. Office building
   B. Warehouse
   C. Multifamily house
   D. All of the above

2. Jack is trying to convince Mary to move to a particular neighborhood because the residents there are of her ethnic background and religion. What is guilty of?

   A. Blockbusting
   B. Discriminating
   C. Convincing
   D. Steering

3. What type of lease would a tenant take when using a warehouse for the purpose of manufacturing and distribution?

   A. Gross lease
   B. Net lease
   C. Percentage lease
   D. Proprietary lease

4. What is a notice given on a pending lawsuit?

   A. Lis Pendens
   B. Statute of limitations
   C. Notice of intent
   D. Notice of default

5. Who issues variances?

   A. Architectural Review Board
   B. EPA
   C. Municipal Engineers
   D. Zoning Board of Appeals

6. What is the name given to an individual who originates, sells and services mortgage loans?

   A. Mortgage Banker
   B. Mortgage Broker
   C. Lender
   D. Borrower

7. What is the exterior layer of a house?

   A. Eaves
   B. Flashing
   C. Pitch
   D. Sheathing

8. Who holds on to the security deposit?

   A. Agent
   B. Broker
   C. Buyer
   D. Landlord

9. What is the term used to define the estimated age of a property based on its utilities and physical wear and tear?

   A. Economic life
   B. Effective age
   C. Use discount
   D. Depreciation

10. How long are brokers required to hold on to property files?

   A. One year
   B. Three years
   C. Five years
   D. Never

11. What is the unit used to measure furnace or air conditioner capacity?

   A. British Thermal Unit
   B. Bytes
   C. Joules
   D. Watts

12. What describes the type of estate granted within a lease?

   A. Acceleration clause
   B. Annuity law
   C. Cancellation clause
   D. Habendum clause

13. What type of income is income generated from a rental property?

   A. Active
   B. Passive
   C. Portfolio
   D. All the above

14. What is another name used to refer to land lease?

   A. Ground lease
   B. Home lease
   C. Percentage lease
   D. Estate lease

15. Which regulations govern the construction details of buildings with the sole interest of safeguarding the occupants and general public?

   A. APR
   B. Building codes
   C. Leasing laws
   D. Zoning codes

16. If a seller nets $325,000 from the sale of her home, and the commission is 3%, how much did the home sell for?

   A. $334,750
   B. $335,051
   C. $315,250
   D. $334,027

17. Personal property that is attached to real property, such as a chandelier, is regarded as

    A. An emblement
    B. An appliance
    C. A fixture
    D. A liability

18. What are outside amenities that maximize use of property called?

    A. Cosmetic improvements
    B. Essential improvements
    C. Offsite improvements
    D. Supplemental improvements

19. Which form of ownership passes the shares of ownership upon death?

    A. Life estate
    B. Severalty
    C. Tenancy in common
    D. Joint tenancy

20. If a property manager is fixing a leaky pipe, what type of maintenance is he doing?

    A. Aesthetic maintenance
    B. Appreciation
    C. Breakdown prevention
    D. Preventive maintenance

21. Which act was enacted in order to identify hazardous sites?

    A. Americans with disabilities Act
    B. CERCLA
    C. Fair Housing Act
    D. Civil Rights Act

22. What is tenancy in common?

    A. A shared tenancy in which each holder has a distinct, separately transferable interest
    B. A tenancy in which each holder has equal interest, where interest is automatically passed in case of death
    C. A tenancy in which interest is returned to the public upon death
    D. A tenancy in which a single owner owns full ownership of a property

23. What is the money available after deducting all expenses?

    A. Cash out returns
    B. Cash flow
    C. Cash on cash return
    D. Revenue

24. What is an involuntary lien?

    A. A lien that arises without the property owner's consent
    B. A lien that is initiated with owner's consent
    C. A lien that cannot be cashed on
    D. None of the above

25. What is the name given to property that legally qualifies as owner's principal property?

   A.   Commercial property
   B.   Homestead property
   C.   Real property
   D.   Personal property

26. A person authorized to handle a principal's affairs in one specific area is referred to as?

   A.   General agent
   B.   Dual agent
   C.   Multi agent
   D.   Special agent

27. What are real property rights conferred with ownership?

   A.   Bundle of rights
   B.   Right of first refusal
   C.   Riparian rights
   D.   Doctrine of equitable conversion

28. What is the fine placed for a violation of license law?

   A. $1,000
   B. $5,000
   C. $6,000
   D. $10,000

29. What is the term for commercial property depreciation?

   A.   5 years
   B.   29 years
   C.   39 years
   D.   40 years

30. The division of expenses at the time of closing between the buyer and seller in proportion to the actual use of a property is called?

   A.   Bill of sale
   B.   Loan to value ratio
   C.   Proration
   D.   Tax abatement

31. What is the equivalent of 1 cubic foot?

   A.   5.25 gallons
   B.   7.26 gallons
   C.   7.48 gallons
   D.   10 gallons

32. What is a statement that shows total revenues generated based on rent rolls and management styles?

   A.   Invoice statement
   B.   Income statement
   C.   Pro forma statement
   D.   Operating statement

33. What type of building is divided into two condominiums where the first is the co-op residential units (80%) and the second is for professional/commercial units (20%)?

    A. Condo
    B. Condop
    C. Co-op
    D. Multi family home

34. A person authorized to handle a principal's affairs in more than one specific area is referred to as?

    A. Special agent
    B. General Agent
    C. Dual agent
    D. Broker

35. What are the laws that limit the maximum interest rate that can be charged?

    A. APR
    B. Annuity laws
    C. FHA
    D. Usury

36. What is the nature of the title in co-op ownership?

    A. Freehold
    B. Leasehold
    C. Regular hold
    D. Lease assignment

37. What is a non-possessory interest in property giving a lienholder the right to foreclose?

    A. Mortgage
    B. Duties
    C. Taxes
    D. Revenue

38. What is the agreement that allows the tenant to continue living on a property once the lease has expired?

    A. Tenancy in common
    B. Tenancy in entirety
    C. Tenancy in sufferance
    D. Ownership in severalty

39. Can a salesperson hold other jobs?

    A. Yes
    B. No
    C. Only if it is in real estate
    D. Maybe

40. What does the Secondary Mortgage Market refer to in the loan process?

    A. Buyers that buy houses on mortgage
    B. Sellers that offer buy down arrangement
    C. Lending market
    D. Private investors and government agencies that buy and sell real estate mortgages

41. What are air rights?

   A.   Right to breath
   B.   Right to own an airspace
   C.   Right to package air
   D.   Rights granted to a property
        owner on the vertical space
        above the property

42. What is the relationship where agents work together in the best interest of their respective clients?

   A.   Dual agency
   B.   Single agency
   C.   Co-broking
   D.   Co-borrowing

43. What is the legal term for passing responsibility of your apartment onto another tenant?

   A.   Sub lease
   B.   Lease assignment
   C.   Leasehold
   D.   Lease break

44. If you have a loan of $200,000 with a 12% interest, how much do you pay in interest every month?

   A. $1,200
   B. $2,000
   C. $2,400
   D. $24,000

45. What are the extra charges above the selling costs that are incurred by the buyer on the purchase of a home?

   A.   Common costs
   B.   Closing costs
   C.   Down payment
   D.   Short fall

46. What are the monthly charges imposed on condo tenants?

   A.   Common charges
   B.   Common costs
   C.   Service fees
   D.   Short fall

47. What is the name given to the ratio defined by dividing monthly debt payments to gross monthly income?

   A.   Loan to value ratio
   B.   Debt to income ratio
   C.   Earnest money deposit
   D.   Foreclosure

48. What is the percentage amount of the selling price that is deposited by the buyer when closing a real estate transaction?

   A.   Down payment
   B.   Escrow
   C.   Earnest money deposit
   D.   Tax abatement

49. What is earnest money deposit?

- A. Money deposited by the buyer to the seller to show interest in the purchase of a home
- B. Purchase money
- C. Down payment
- D. Security deposit

50. What is the financial agreement that allows a third party to regulate payment where two parties are involved?

- A. Security deposit
- B. Sales deposit
- C. Escrow
- D. Earnest money deposit

51. What is the notice given when a tenant is in violation of the lease agreement and is up for eviction?

- A. Notice to cure
- B. Notice of intention
- C. Notice of termination
- D. Notice to quit

52. What is the notice given when a squatter is accommodated without the landlord's consent?

- A. Notice of default
- B. Notice of intention
- C. Notice to cure
- D. Notice to quit

53. What is the notice given to state that no work has been performed?

- A. Notice of cessation
- B. Notice given to evict an unruly tenant
- C. Notice filed in court by a lender on defaulting of payment
- D. Notice to discontinue the breach of lease within 10 days

54. What is the name given to a visit made to a potential property to identify the condition of the house?

- A. Final walk through
- B. Home inspection
- C. Appraisal
- D. Assessment

55. What mortgage plan allows a borrower to switch to a fixed-rate mortgage?

- A. Adjustable rate Mortgage
- B. Convertible ARM
- C. Fixed rate mortgage
- D. Floating rate mortgage

56. What is the situation that arises when an individual that is legally required to make payments does not fulfill this obligation?

- A. Delinquency
- B. Defaulting
- C. Escalation clause
- D. Foreclosure

57. Which agency insures FHA-approved lenders?

   A. CERCLA
   B. Consumer Financial Protection Bureau
   C. Federal Emergency Management Agency
   D. Federal Housing Administration

58. Which agency is commissioned with overseeing products and services offered to consumers in the finance industry?

   A. Consumer Financial Protection Bureau
   B. Federal Housing Administration
   C. Environmental Protection Agency
   D. Federal Emergency Management Agency

59. What service allows brokers to share their listings?

   A. Broker Listing Service
   B. Single Agency Listing
   C. Multiple Listing Service
   D. Shared Listing Service

60. What is the contract covering household maintenance systems?

   A. Deed
   B. Home warranty
   C. Hazard insurance
   D. HO4

61. What is the name given to a real estate transaction where buyers outbid each other for the property?

   A. Acceleration clause
   B. Escalation clause
   C. Public auction
   D. Tender

62. What is the name given to a notice given showing interest in a property?

   A. Notice of cessation
   B. Notice to cure
   C. Notice of default
   D. Notice of intent

63. What is the increase in the value of a property?

   A. Appreciation
   B. Depreciation
   C. Obsolescence
   D. All of the above

64. What is the mortgage payment plan that involves making payments every fortnight?

   A. Balloon mortgage
   B. Biweekly mortgage
   C. Blanket mortgage
   D. Graduated mortgage

65. What term is used to describe the document attached to an original contract?

   A.   Addendum
   B.   Signed agreement
   C.   Requirements clause
   D.   Terms and conditions

66. What refinancing method allows a borrower to acquire cash from the transaction?

   A.   Cash flow
   B.   Cash out refinance
   C.   Cash on cash return
   D.   Refinancing

67. Who oversees that code restrictions are followed and construction / renovation are done by licensed professionals?

   A.   Contractor
   B.   Department of Buildings
   C.   Zoning board
   D.   Architectural Review Board

68. What is the final stage of a real estate transaction?

   A.   Closing
   B.   Sale
   C.   Final walk through
   D.   Handing of the title

69. What is the percentage of the selling price that is usually earned by a real estate agent for facilitating the transaction?

   A.   Bonus
   B.   Commission
   C.   Salary
   D.   Rent

70. What is the name of fees paid to the lender at closing in exchange for a reduced interest rate?

   A.   Mortgage
   B.   Service fee
   C.   Discount points
   D.   Principal fee

71. Which Act was passed to protect against discrimination in borrowing?

   A.   Equal Credit Opportunity Act
   B.   Fair and Accurate Credit Transaction Act of 2003
   C.   The Fair Credit Reporting Act
   D.   Truth in Lending Act

72. What does the phrase "For Sale by Owner" mean?

   A.   A sale is being facilitated by an agent
   B.   Investors are open to receiving offers
   C.   A property sale is being handled without a real estate agent
   D.   All of the above

73. What is the name of the document used to summarize all the fees incurred by the lender and borrower during settlement of a loan?

    A.   Financial statement
    B.   Invoice
    C.   IOU
    D.   Settlement statement

74. Which entity determines the assessed value of a property?

    A.   Building Inspector
    B.   Municipal council
    C.   Real estate agent
    D.   Tax assessor

75. If a property is taxed at 40% with a tax levy of $88,000, what is its assessed value?

    A. $220,000
    B. $146,666
    C. $123,200
    D.   None of the above

76. Which type of estate has rights to the property for an indefinite duration?

    A.   List estate
    B.   Estate for years
    C.   Freehold estate
    D.   Less-than-freehold estate

77. Which of the following is **not** an essential element of a deed?

    A.   Signature of the grantee
    B.   Date
    C.   Identification of the grantor and grantee
    D.   Adequate description of the property

78. What is a lessor?

    A.   A person who leases real estate property from the owner of said property
    B.   A person that makes a grant
    C.   The owner of real estate who leases the property to another
    D.   The person who transfers property by sale

79. What is the definition of a joint tenancy?

    A.   When property is held by two or more parties
    B.   When a third party trust owns the property
    C.   When the seller and the buyer both own the property
    D.   When the property is inherited by a family member

80. What is the definition of a trust deed?

    A.   The owner of the real estate property who leases the property to another
    B.   A deed with limited or no warranties
    C.   A deed that transfers property to a family member
    D.   A document used when one party has taken out a loan from another party to purchase property

81. _____ refers to land and buildings that need to be held for a long period of time to pay for themselves.

- A. Fixity
- B. Nonhomogeneity
- C. Situs
- D. Datum

82. A shop owner leases a space in a strip mall for 2 years. The strip mall is sold to a new owner during the duration of the lease. What is the status of the lease?

- A. The lease is void
- B. The new property owner and tenant must honor all the terms of the original lease
- C. The new property owner has the right to make changes to the lease within 30 days of the sale
- D. The lease starts fresh with the new property owner as the landlord

83. A homeowner's association does not allow owners to have pets. This is an example of a _____ clause.

- A. Possessions
- B. Contingency
- C. Restricted covenants
- D. Defeasance

84. Tenancy by the entirety is only applicable to _____.

- A. Homeowners with an FHA loan
- B. Low income homeowners
- C. Recently divorced couples
- D. Married couples

85. A building inspector must provide a(an) _____ before the property can be used.

   A. Certificate of occupancy
   B. Quitclaim deed
   C. Pre-qualification
   D. Examination of title

86. Which of the following is a type of zoning?

   A. Rural
   B. Business
   C. Vacation
   D. Landmark

87. A _____ is a real estate professional that performs a visual survey of a property's structure.

   A. Developer
   B. Broker
   C. Real estate appraiser
   D. Home inspector

88. Which of the following is an example of a special purpose real property?

   A. Farm
   B. Public school
   C. Timeshare
   D. Condominium

89. _____ is the 2ⁿᵈ largest purchaser of the secondary market and buys mainly FHA and VA loans.

    A. Federal National Mortgage Association
    B. U.S. Housing and Urban Development
    C. Government National Mortgage Association
    D. Federal Housing Administration loan

90. Which of the following is not an economic characteristic of land?

    A. Scarcity
    B. Permanence of investment
    C. Size
    D. Improvements

91. A _____ is a provision in a mortgage that can make the debt immediately due if the borrower sells the property.

    A. Acceleration clause
    B. Alienation clause
    C. Prepayment clause
    D. Defeasance clause

92. Which survey system was adopted in 1785, and is also called the Public Land Survey System or Rectangular Survey System?

    A. Geographic Information System
    B. Tallahassee Meridian
    C. Government Survey System
    D. Principal Meridian

93. What is condemnation?

    A. The right the government has to acquire privately owned property for public use

    B. Occurs when the government seizes private property and compensates the owner

    C. Occurs when the government seizes private property and does not compensate the owner

    D. The right the government has to take privately owned property for private use

94. Which organization purchases conventional loans from savings and loans to promote stability and affordability in the housing market?

    A. Federal Home Loan Mortgage Corporation

    B. U.S. Housing and Urban Development

    C. Federal Housing Administration

    D. National Realtors Association

95. Which factors affect the demand of real estate?

    A. Population

    B. Employment

    C. Demographics

    D. All of the above

96. Which rights give the owner the right to access water when property is adjacent to a lake or an ocean?

    A. Littoral rights

    B. Riparian rights

    C. Quitclaim deed

    D. Easement

97. A _____ is a process that releases the borrower from the obligation of debt once all mortgage payment terms are met.

    A. Acceleration clause
    B. Defeasance clause
    C. Alienation clause
    D. None of the above

98. Also called restrictive covenants, this limits how a piece of real estate can be used.

    A. Reconveyance
    B. Zoning ordinances
    C. Deed restrictions
    D. Arbitration

99. Which legal document establishes one debt as inferior to another debt for collecting repayment from a debtor?

    A. Purchase agreement
    B. Closing disclosure
    C. Property deed
    D. Subordination agreement

100. Which law requires financial institutions to maintain, report and disclose loan information regarding mortgages?

    A. Home Mortgage Disclosure Act
    B. Community Reinvestment Act
    C. Real Estate Settlement Procedures Act
    D. Truth in Lending Act

THIS IS THE END OF THE NATIONAL PORTION.

State Portion

1. North Carolina has a _____ statutory redemption period after the auction of a foreclosed property.

   A. 10 days
   B. 1 year
   C. 6 months
   D. 90 days

2. North Carolina is a _____ state which means a lender has the right to foreclose on property without going to court.

   A. Non-court
   B. Judicial foreclosure
   C. Non-judicial foreclosure
   D. Power of sale

3. Which of the following is true about the first deed of trust in North Carolina?

   A. They are not exempt from state usury laws
   B. They are exempt from state usury laws
   C. Only some state usury laws are exempt
   D. None of the above

4. Which of the following cannot be charged a prepayment penalty in North Carolina?

   A. A residential loan with an original balance of $150,000
   B. An FHA loan
   C. A VA loan
   D. All of the above

5. The procedure for foreclosing a _____ is simpler and faster because there is an automatic power-of-sale clause in it.

    A.   North Carolina deed of trust
    B.   Title theory
    C.   Foreclosure clause
    D.   Default clause

6. When a mortgagor gives the legal title to the mortgagee and retains equitable title _____ is being exercised.

    A.   Mortgagee responsibility act
    B.   North Carolina title theory
    C.   Equitable title theory
    D.   None of the above

7. Property taxes are legally due on the _____ of each year in North Carolina.

    A.   1st of September
    B.   1st of January
    C.   31st of December
    D.   1st of July

8. To allow a landlocked owner the right of ingress and egress over a grantor's land is called _____.

    A.   Easement in gross
    B.   Easement by prescription
    C.   Easement appurtenant
    D.   Easement by necessity

9. A property owner extends a structure on to the neighbor's property. This is called _____.

   A. Appurtenance
   B. Encroachment
   C. Blockbusting
   D. Commingling

10. Which type of co-ownership does not include the right to survivorship?

   A. Tenancy by the entirety
   B. Non-survivorship tenancy
   C. Tenancy in common
   D. Tenements

11. How many years does a person need to use another person's property to gain an easement by prescription in North Carolina?

   A. 20 years
   B. 10 years
   C. 6 months
   D. 1 year

12. When a court retains custody of an owner's unsecured property, at the request of a creditor, it is called a _____.

   A. Writ of attachment
   B. Writ of execution
   C. Commingling
   D. None of the above

13. A paving company paves a dirt road that runs adjacent to your property. A(n) _____ tax will be placed to pay for such an infrastructure project.

    A. Ad valorem property
    B. Personal property
    C. The owners affected would have to pay for it
    D. Special assessment

14. A property owner uses a neighbor's driveway to get to work every day. The property owner has an easement over the driveway. The neighbor's driveway is called a(n) _____.

    A. Leasehold estate
    B. Pur autre vie estate
    C. Servient estate
    D. Dominant estate

15. All of the following are types of easements except _____.

    A. Appurtenant
    B. Assessment
    C. By necessity
    D. By prescription

16. When a HOA limits an owner to the size home they are able to build it is called _____.

    A. Property limits
    B. HOA rights
    C. Deed restrictions
    D. A HOA does not have the right to do such a thing

17. If a co-owner of real estate property passes, and the other co-owners automatically receive the deceased owner's title this is called _____.

   A. Right of co-ownership
   B. Survivorship
   C. Joint ownership
   D. There is no such law, the ownership would go to the next of kin

18. The right to have land supported from below is called _____.

   A. Subjacent support
   B. Lateral support
   C. Bilateral support
   D. Surface support

19. Why should a deed be recorded?

   A. There is no reason to record a deed
   B. For tax purposes
   C. To establish priority of real property ownership interests between individuals with competing claims
   D. None of the above

20. When real estate is owned by a single person it is called _____. This word is also derived from the face that the owner is served from other owners.

   A. Joint ownership
   B. Entireties
   C. Severalty
   D. There is no such type of ownership

21. The rights an owner has to a river that is adjoining their property is called _____.

    A. Riparian rights
    B. Littoral rights
    C. Water rights
    D. Freehold rights

22. The practice of a debtor pledging collateral to secure debt is called _____.

    A. Hypothecation
    B. Commingling
    C. Arbitration
    D. None of the above

23. _____ is when a title is returned to the holder of a future interest.

    A. Return deed
    B. Reversionary interest
    C. Reversionary deed
    D. None of the above

24. Which of the following is an example of a unilateral contract?

    A. Mortgage
    B. Deed of trust
    C. Notes
    D. All of the above

25. This type of foreclosure allows a lender to buy a deed.

    A.   Friendly foreclosure
    B.   Judgement foreclosure
    C.   Voluntary foreclosure
    D.   There is no such foreclosure

26. A VA loan is non assumable unless there is approval from _____.

    A.   A judge ruling
    B.   The veterans affairs
    C.   NCREC
    D.   Any of the above

27. A _____ is a condensed history of a title to a specific parcel of real estate.

    A.   Color title
    B.   Abstract of title
    C.   Summary of title
    D.   Title history

28. What clause in a mortgage states that the entire debt is due immediately if the borrower defaults on an installment payment?

    A.   Defeasance clause
    B.   Default clause
    C.   Acceleration clause
    D.   No such clause exists

29. Acceptance or the expression of interest by the offeree to be bound by the terms of the offer, must be _____.

   A. In writing
   B. Verbal or in writing
   C. Notarized
   D. Signed by a witness

30. When there is an increase of land on property due to the deposit of sand or soil being washed by naturally from a water source, it is called _____.

   A. Accrued land
   B. Riparian
   C. Littoral
   D. Accretion

31. What is a constructive eviction?

   A. When a tenant is physically removed from property
   B. When a landlord deprives the tenant use of a portion of the leased premises
   C. When a landlord fails to provide the necessary services
   D. All of the above are constructive eviction

32. Which of the following is needed to claim adverse possession?

   A. Open possession of another's land
   B. Continuous possession of another's land
   C. Exclusive possession of another's land
   D. All of the above

33. When the exterior color of real property is regulated due to zoning ordinances, this is also called _____.

    A. Residential zoning
    B. Aesthetic zoning
    C. Historic zoning
    D. Commercial zoning

34. The relationship between a principal and an agent where the agent has authority to represent the principal in certain transactions is called a(n) _____.

    A. Agency
    B. Agreement
    C. Commingling
    D. None of the above

35. A(n) _____ is a clause that requires the lender's approval to all another party to assume the debt from the borrower.

    A. Acceleration clause
    B. Alienation clause
    C. Borrower clause
    D. There is no such clause

36. A change to contractual terms or conditions is a(n) _____.

    A. Change clause
    B. Commingling
    C. Blockbusting
    D. Addendum

37. _____ is the addition to property by attaching a smaller item to a larger piece of property.

    A. Commingling
    B. Addendum
    C. Annexation
    D. None of the above

38. A(n) _____ is when a tenant is physically removed from land or rental property.

    A. Actual eviction
    B. Constructive eviction
    C. Partial eviction
    D. Physical eviction

39. A lawsuit that aims to silence challenges or claims to a title is called a _____.

    A. Action to silence title
    B. Silence title
    C. Title claim
    D. Action to quiet title

40. A property owner's land has been naturally detached and has attached to another property owner's land. This is called _____.

    A. Accretion
    B. Avulsion
    C. Riparian
    D. Littoral

THIS IS THE END OF THE STATE PORTION.

Answer Key – National Portion

1.	D	21.	B	41.	D	61.	B	81.	A
2.	D	22.	A	42.	C	62.	D	82.	B
3.	B	23.	B	43.	B	63.	A	83.	C
4.	A	24.	A	44.	B	64.	B	84.	D
5.	D	25.	B	45.	B	65.	A	85.	A
6.	A	26.	D	46.	A	66.	B	86.	A
7.	D	27.	A	47.	B	67.	B	87.	D
8.	D	28.	A	48.	A	68.	A	88.	B
9.	B	29.	C	49.	A	69.	B	89.	C
10.	B	30.	C	50.	C	70.	C	90.	C
11.	A	31.	C	51.	C	71.	A	91.	B
12.	D	32.	D	52.	D	72.	C	92.	C
13.	B	33.	B	53.	A	73.	D	93.	B
14.	A	34.	B	54.	B	74.	D	94.	A
15.	B	35.	D	55.	B	75.	A	95.	D
16.	B	36.	B	56.	A	76.	C	96.	A
17.	C	37.	A	57.	D	77.	A	97.	B
18.	C	38.	C	58.	A	78.	C	98.	C
19.	D	39.	A	59.	C	79.	A	99.	D
20.	D	40.	D	60.	B	80.	D	100.	A

1.   **D) All of the above**

Commercial property includes mixed use buildings (e.g. retail store on the first floor, residences above) office buildings, hotels, retail stores, multifamily houses, industrial warehouses, and more.

2.   **D) Steering**

Steering is the act of guiding prospective buyers to specified settlement areas based on race, religion and other discriminatory factors.

3.   **B) Net lease**

This is a lease where the tenant pays rent and part of utilities fee and property taxes. The landlord is tasked with paying the utility bills and property taxes that are not covered by the tenant. This lease is common in commercial real estate.

4. **A) Lis Pendens**

This is a legal notice that a lawsuit concerning a real estate property is pending. Usually involves a property title or claims of ownership interest. Details of a property whose title is in question are required to be filed at the county record to notify future buyers and lenders.

5. **D) Zoning Board of Appeals**

The Zoning Board of Appeals is a board of select members that is given jurisdiction to hear and decide on appeals regarding zoning laws.

6. **A) Mortgage Banker**

A mortgage banker is an individual who originates, closes and funds with his own funds or that of a company. Once a mortgage is originated it is either retained or sold to an investor. A mortgage banker has the power to approve or reject a mortgage and earns fees on the origination of a loan.

7. **D) Sheathing**

Sheathing is a covering structure and acts as a case for the exterior of the home. Usually used to describe a boarding material that forms the roof, floor and walls. It provides a surface for other materials and strengthens weather resistance.

8. **D) Landlord**

A security deposit is an amount equaling monthly rent that is paid to ensure rent will be paid and to cater for other responsibilities highlighted in the lease. Can also be used as security for unpaid rent and damages and is held onto by the landlord.

9. **B) Effective age**

This is an estimate of a building age based on its utilities and the wear and tear. It could be the actual age or a little more or less than the actual age. This is dependent on maintenance, remodeling and removal of inadequacies. It is used to determine the remaining life of a building.

10. **B) Three years**

Brokers are required by law to hold on to a copy of property files for a minimum of 3 years. This is to act as a proof in case of a dispute in the future. These include copies of all listings, deposit receipts, cancelled checks and trust records executed or obtained during the transaction.

11.   **A) British Thermal Unit**

Defined as the amount of heat required to raise the temperature of one pound of water by one degree Fahrenheit. In the case of air conditioning, it is defined as the number of BTU per hour products that can be added or removed from the air.

12.   **D) Habendum clause**

This is a legal agreement that involves the rights and interests of a property being transferred to a lessee. For a leased property there is a transfer of ownership and restrictions on the property. A purchased property is void of restrictions and only transfers ownership.

13.   **B) Passive**

This is an income source that requires little to no daily input in order to yield returns.

14.   **A) Ground lease**

This is a lease agreement where a tenant is allowed to develop a parcel of land during the lease period. On expiry of the lease, all improvements remain in the owner's custody. Land leases are often last between 50-99 with other agreement allowing for renewal.

15.   **B) Building codes**

These are a set of regulations that are put in place to ensure design, construction, alteration and maintenance of structures is done according to the state's requirements. They aim at safeguarding the health, safety and welfare of the occupants.

16.   **B) $335,051**

$325,000 / (1 - 0.03) = $335,051

17.   **C) A fixture**

A fixture is any physical property that is permanently attached to real property (usually land). Fixtures are treated as a part of real property. Examples of fixtures are ceiling fans and TV mounts.

18.   **C) Offsite improvements**

Offsite improvements are amenities that are not within the premise of the structure but are necessary to maximize the use of the property and ultimately increase the value of the property.

19.   **D) Joint tenancy**

Joint tenancy is a form of ownership in which several people own a property together, each with equal shares and rights. If one of the owners in a joint tenancy dies, that owner's share in the property is automatically passed to the remaining owners.

20.   **D) Preventive maintenance**

In order to maintain tenants and an acceptable return on an investment, routine checks and repairs have to be done. These are done to safeguard against failing which may incur losses to the property manager that arise due to cost of replacement.

21.   **B) CERCLA**

The Comprehensive Environmental Response Compensation and Liability Act of 1980 was enacted in order to identify, investigate and facilitate cleanup of hazardous sites. The act is currently administered by the Environmental Protection Agency.

22.   **A) A shared tenancy in which each holder has a distinct, separately transferable interest**

This type of ownership is characterized by ownership between two or more people who can have either equal or unequal shares. Unlike a joint tenancy, if an owner dies, the person's share is passed to his/her heirs and not distributed to the remaining owners.

23.   **B) Cash flow**

This is the amount of profit retained after paying off all operating costs and repurposing amounts made in dividends for use in future repairs. To be able to profit from an investment, one must maintain a positive cash flow.

24.   **A) A lien that arises without the property owner's consent**

Involuntary liens are placed by government facilities for unpaid taxes.

25.   **B) Homestead property**

Homestead laws are laws that exist to ensure to protect owners from losing their home equity while filing for bankruptcy. Homestead property enables an individual to declare a portion of property as homestead to avoid forced sale.

26.   **D) Special agent**

This is an agent engaged to perform a specific duty for a client. Their authority is limited to that particular task that translates in the expiry of the contract once the task is completed.

27. **A) Bundle of rights**

These are legal rights that are granted to a property buyer which include right to possession, control, exclusion, enjoyment and disposition. A property owner is automatically granted the bundle of rights. In a commercial property, different rights can be assigned to different parties.

28. **A) $1,000**

Violation of license laws may result in suspension of a license or a fine of not more than $1,000 paid to the Department of State. A reprimand is given together with the fine.

29. **C) 39 years**

After 39 years a commercial property is eligible for applying for value loss by depreciation in order to reduce property taxes levied

30. **C) Proration**

Proration occurs during corporate action to ensure all shareholders are treated fairly and a company does not deviate from its original target. Shareholders are offered equity or cash and required to elect one. Once the election is done, shareholders are compensated and if the shares or cash are not enough to satisfy the election each shareholder gets their due in both equity and cash.

31. **C) 7.48 gallons**

32. **D) Operating statement**

An operating statement is a financial statement that is done monthly and annually to document the expenses incurred and revenue gained. From the statement one can calculate the net profit or loss within the period.

33. **B) Condop**

This is a real estate building where the housing units are divided into co-op residential units and condos. They offer more flexible rules than a co-op. Condo units are retained or sold separately by the developer.

34. **B) General Agent**

This is an agent that is mandated to represent the principal in more than one affair.

35. **D) Usury**

These are laws that are laws set in place to protect borrowers from abusive lending such as imposing unusually high interest rates. Lenders usually target with little knowledge on the traditional loan system. An APR is usually set to protect buyers from being exploited by lenders.

36. **B) Leasehold**

This is a title on a property being leased and scheduled payments are made throughout the term of the lease. Improvements made within the property are either expensed or capitalized depending on their values.

37. **A) Mortgage**

A mortgage is a voluntary lien taken out to raise funds to buy a property. The lien is entered willingly and therefore possession of the property remains with the debtor.

38. **C) Tenancy in sufferance**

In this case, a tenant is granted the privilege to live within the premise before landlord decides to ask the tenant to vacate. Terms of the original lease must be met during this period of time. This type of tenancy can only be terminated by a written notice given not less than 30 days before the tenant is expected to move out.

39. **A) Yes**

There are no laws restricting a real estate salesperson from working multiple jobs.

40. **D) Private investors and government agencies that buy and sell real estate mortgages**

This is where home loans and servicing rights are bought within the market. Once a home loan is obtained, it is underwritten, financed and services by a lending facility. A lending facility sells loans to the secondary mortgage market in order to replenish loaning money.

41. **D) Rights granted to a property owner on the vertical space above the property**

The air space is subject to reasonable use by neighboring buildings and aircrafts. Like with property, air rights can be leased or sold.

42. **C) Co-broking**

This is a situation where two or more agents that are involved in the same the same transaction agree to work together in order to meet the needs of both parties. In this case, the agents are legally required to act in the best interest of the clients.

43. **B) Lease assignment**

A lease assignment is a legal arrangement where the landlord allows a tenant to assign another tenant to lease the apartment. The tenant is responsible for paying rent and utility fees directly to the landlord. In the case of a lease assignment, the previous tenant is held accountable for defaults in unpaid bills by the assignee.

44. **B) $2,000**

($200,000 * 0.12) / 12 = $2,000

45. **B) Closing costs**

These are the extra costs that are usually incurred by a home buyer on top the agreed upon price. They usually include title insurance, attorney fees and lender fees. These costs are negotiable but commonly paid by buyers.

46. **A) Common charges**

These are the monthly charges that are imposed on condo and condop tenants to cover common charges and amenities. They are usually cover maintenance of shared spaces and operation expenses of a building.

47. **B) Debt to income ratio**

This is a way lenders calculate the ability of a borrower to manage the monthly payments required in the settlement plan. Borrowers with a higher ratio have been established to experience struggles in meeting the monthly payments. 43% has been determined to be the highest ratio that can be offered credit.

48. **A) Down payment**

A down payment is an amount paid by the buyer to the seller to secure the property. A down payment is usually paid from the buyer's savings. Contrary to common belief, there is no set percentage of down payment that should be placed on a property

49. **A) Money deposited by the buyer to the seller to show interest in the purchase of a home**

This amount is deposited to give the buyer time to look into the title, sanction an appraisal and conduct an inspection of the property. This money can be returned to the buyer only in the case of a contract breach.

50.   **C) Escrow**

This arrangement involves a third party that is neutral to the transaction. Usually used to secure payment in an account that can only be released on meeting of all the terms of the agreement. An escrow account is often used in transactions that involve large amounts of money such as real estate. A listing agent open an account and once the terms are signed upon by both the buyer and the seller, the deal is closed.

51.   **C) Notice of termination**

This is a notice given to a tenant to end tenancy stating the reason for termination of tenancy, the date by which the tenant is required to vacate the premise and the legal implication of refusing to move.

52.   **D) Notice to quit**

This is a notice given by the landlord regarding someone living in the home as a squatter. The notice usually states that the tenant is required to vacate the property within 10 days and the implications of failing to do so.

53.   **A) Notice of cessation**

This is notice given by the contractor by the contractee to state that no work regarding construction has been done for a specified period of time. This notice is given in order to begin mechanical liens compensation.

54.   **B) Home inspection**

They are an important part of the real estate transaction as one is able to identify the condition of the property being bought. Inspection of facilities such as plumbing, fixtures and foundation condition comes in handy in determining the value of the property.

55.   **B) Convertible ARM**

This is a mortgage plan that allows an individual to benefit from the falling interest rates with the option of switching to a fixed-rate payment plan at a small fee. This switch can be made within the second to fifth year of the mortgage payment period.

56.   **A) Delinquency**

This is a situation that arises where a borrower that is legally bound with the responsibility to make necessary payments on a loan or a bond interest foregoes paying the loan. Delinquency usually results in penalties depending on the type of loan and reasons behind failed payments.

57. **D) Federal Housing Administration**

This is United States Agency whose goal is to enable low income individual acquire mortgage loans. The agency approves and insures the lenders. An FHA loan requires a loan down payment and a credit score of at least 580.

58. **A) Consumer Financial Protection Bureau**

This is a regulatory agency that is tasked with the responsibility of overseeing the products and services offered to consumers by financial institutions. In the event of mishandling of a consumer, a complaint is filed to the CFPB for resolution.

59. **C) Multiple Listing Service**

This is a system employed by real estate broker that allows them to view each other's listings. Sharing the database amongst a group of brokers enables brokers to identify buyers for properties they are engaged in.

60. **B) Home warranty**

This is a contract made to ensure the cost of maintaining a household are met. It is put in place as a legal assurance that the property is fit for its intended purpose and meets the expectations of the buyer. It is usually taken to protect against expensive home repairs.

61. **B) Escalation clause**

This is a contract that allows a buyer to set a selling price but any offers higher than the stated price will automatically lead to an increase in the set price. This gives sellers an option to outbid each other and help in making the decision for the sale price.

62. **D) Notice of intent**

This is a non-binding proposal between a buyer and seller of a property to negotiate terms of a real estate transaction. It is usually detailed and lays key points on the weight of the transaction. It is usually used to determine the seriousness of the prospective buyer on the property.

63. **A) Appreciation**

This is the increase in the value of an asset over a period of time. It usually occurs due to increased demand or weakening supply.

64. **B) Biweekly mortgage**

This is a mortgage that requires a principal and interest payment plan every two weeks. It usually has a reduced interest rate throughout the lifespan of the loan.

65. **A) Addendum**

This is an attached document that is usually included as part of the contract during the preparation. It can act as an informal explanatory attachment or to indicate other requirements of the contract that have not been included in the main attachment.

66. **B) Cash out refinance**

This is where a homeowner refinances a mortgage for more than its value and withdraws the difference amount as cash. It is only possible to borrowers with a 20% equity on their mortgage.

67. **B) Department of Buildings**

In order to ensure that building codes are adhered to and construction and renovations are done by professionals, a building permit is required for any building or renovation project. A building permit is a go ahead issued by local government to a contractor to construct or remodel a building. It is issued to ensure that building codes are adhered to and standards are maintained.

68. **A) Closing**

This is the final stage of a real estate transaction. At this point, the date where contract becomes active is agreed on. On the closing date, the property is legally transferred from the seller to the buyer.

69. **B) Commission**

This is the percentage earned by a real estate agent for effort placed in facilitating the transaction. It is usually between 5-6% of the sales price and is paid by the seller on closing. It is usually split between the buyer's and seller's agent.

70. **C) Discount points**

Also referred to as mortgage points, these are fees paid directly to a lender by a homebuyer at closing time. They are usually paid in exchange for lower interest rates reducing monthly payments on the mortgage.

71. **A) Equal Credit Opportunity Act**

This act was enacted in 1974 and rules it unlawful for lenders to discriminate against loan applicants based on gender, race, age and religion.

72.   **C) A property sale is being handled without a real estate agent**

This phrase is used to declare that a property sale is being handled without a real estate agent. While using real estate agents to facilitate sale, some home sellers would rather avoid agents in order to save on the amount spent on commission. In this case the seller must disclose that they are not using an agent.

73.   **D) Settlement statement**

This is a document that is usually used to summarize expenses incurred during a loan translation and varies according to loan types. It is usually part of the closing package that must be reviewed and signed by the borrower when closing a loan. A comprehensive settlement statement is legally required for every loan.

74.   **D) Tax assessor**

An official whose responsibility is to determine the value of each taxable property in a region.

75.   **A) $220,000**

$88,000 / 0.4 = $220,000

76.   **C) Freehold estate**

An estate that has exclusive rights of the property for an undefined length of time. The three types of freehold estates are fee simple absolute, fee simple defeasible and life estate.

77.   **A) Signature of the grantee**

The grantee does not need to sign a deed. A deed needs to be in writing, must be signed by the grantor, the grantor must have the legal capacity to transfer the property, the grantor and grantee must be identified, the property must be described adequately, the deed must be legally delivered to the grantee and the grantee must accept the deed.

78.   **C) The owner of real estate who leases the property to another**

A person who grants a lease to someone else. This person is the owner of the real estate and leases it a lessee through an agreement.

79.   **A) When property is held by two or more parties**

It is an agreement in which two or more people own a property with equal rights and obligations. Joint tenancy is typically entered at the same time and through a deed. If one of the owners were to die their portion of the property would automatically pass to the survivors.

80. **D) A document used when one party has taken out a loan from another party to purchase property**

It represents an agreement between the borrower and the lender in which the property is held in a trust managed by a third party until the borrower pays off the loan. The legal title of the property is transferred to the third party to hold. Trust deeds are used in place of mortgages in numerous states.

81. **A) Fixity**

Also called investment permanence is property that takes a long time to pay for itself. It also refers to the fact that land cannot be moved but is in a fixed location.

82. **B) The new property owner and tenant must honor all the terms of the original lease**

Property sold with an existing lease is still valid and it must be honored by both the new owner and the tenant.

83. **C) Restrictive covenants**

Restrictive covenants are restrictions on land use to ensure the value and enjoyment of adjoining land will be preserved. This clause limits what a tenant or owner can do with property.

84. **D) Married couples**

Tenancy by the entirety is a type of concurrent estate in real property limited to married couples. Each spouse has an equal and undivided interest in the property and they mutually own the entire estate.

85. **A) Certificate of occupancy**

A building inspector must issue a certificate of occupancy after the final inspection. It is a document issued by the local government or building department that states the building is in compliance with the building codes and is suitable for occupancy.

86. **A) Rural**

There are numerous different types of zoning: rural, residential, commercial, industrial, agricultural, combination and historic.

87. **D) Home inspector**

A home inspector determines the condition of the structure. A home inspection is a non-invasive examination of the home condition and should not be confused with an appraisal which determines the value of the property.

88. **B) Public school**

   Public schools are an example of special purpose property. It is property that is appropriate for one type of use and has a unique design. It uses special construction materials and other features which limit the use of the property.

89. **C) Government National Mortgage Association**

   The GNMA guarantees the timely payment of principal and interest on mortgage-backed securities that have been issued by approved lenders. It is also referred to as Ginnie Mae.

90. **C) Size**

   Size is not an economic characteristic of land. The economic characteristics of land are factors that affect its value in the marketplace. These are scarcity, improvements, performance of investment and location.

91. **B) Alienation clause**

   This clause states that the borrower needs to pay the mortgage in full before the borrower can transfer the property to another person. This clause will go into effect whether the property is transferred voluntarily or involuntarily.

92. **C) Government Survey System**

   This system identifies reference lines and makes up townships and sections. It has been applied to most of the land in the United States since its adoption in 1785.

93. **B) Occurs when the government seizes private property and compensates the owner**

   Condemnation occurs when the government acquires land through eminent domain. Eminent domain is the right the government has to acquire privately owned property for public use.

94. **A) Federal Home Loan Mortgage Corporation**

   This organization was created by the congress but is not a government agency and does not receive government funding. It is owned by shareholders and overseen by its board of directors.

95. **D) All of the above**

   The factors that affect demand are population, demographics, employment interest rates and borrowing costs.

96. **A) Littoral rights**

These rights are considered water rights that concern bodies of water that are static like an ocean, lake or bay. Rights for flowing water are determined by the riparian rights.

97. **B) Defeasance clause**

This clause states that a borrower will be given the title to the property once the mortgage payment terms are met. It is the final procedures in a mortgage contract.

98. **C) Deed restrictions**

Deeds restrictions are a clause in a deed that limits how real estate can be used and what can be built on the land. Most often the restrictions are not covered by community zoning regulations.

99. **D) Subordination agreement**

This agreement comes up when a home has a first and a second mortgage and the borrower would like to refinance the first mortgage. It adjusts the priority of the new loan.

100. **A) Home Mortgage Disclosure Act**

This law is used to monitor the geographic targets of mortgage lenders, provides mechanisms for predatory lending practices and provides reporting statistics on the mortgage market to the government.

Answer Key – State Portion

1.	A	21.	A
2.	C	22.	A
3.	B	23.	B
4.	D	24.	D
5.	A	25.	A
6.	B	26.	B
7.	A	27.	B
8.	D	28.	C
9.	B	29.	A
10.	C	30.	D
11.	A	31.	C
12.	A	32.	D
13.	D	33.	B
14.	C	34.	A
15.	B	35.	B
16.	C	36.	D
17.	B	37.	C
18.	A	38.	A
19.	C	39.	D
20.	C	40.	B

1. **A) 10 days**

In this ten-day period, the borrower can repurchase the home by filing an upset bit. The bid must be 5% more than the foreclosure sale price.

2. **C) Non-judicial foreclosure**

This is done through a power-of-sale clause that gives the lender the right to foreclose on property without a court order.

3. **B) They are exempt from state usury laws**

These are laws that regulate the amount for interest that can be charged on a loan. These laws specifically target the practice of charging excessively high rates on loans by setting caps on maximum interest that can be levied.

4. **D) All of the above**

All of the above are situations in which a lender in North Carolina cannot charge a prepayment penalty on a residential loan.

5. **A) North Carolina deed of trust**

This a three-party security instrument is in lieu of a mortgage and makes it simpler for a foreclosure to occur if the borrower defaults.

6. **B) North Carolina title theory**

This gives the legal title to the mortgagee and retains equitable title. The mortgagor receives the title when the debt is paid in full.

7. **A) 1st of September**

North Carolina's property tax due date is the 1st of September. The last day taxes can be paid without penalty is January 5th.

8. **D) Easement by necessity**

This type of easement is allowed by law and is necessary for an owner to fully enjoy a parcel of real estate.

9. **B) Encroachment**

This is an unauthorized intrusion of an improvement or any part of an improvement on the real property of another person. This can make the title to both parcels unmarketable and is best discovered by a survey.

10. **C) Tenancy in common**

In this type of ownership, there is no right to survivorship. This is a way for two people to co-own property without survivorship.

11. **A) 20 years**

North Carolina requires a person to adversely use property for 20 or more years to gain easement of that property.

12. **A) Writ of attachment**

A creditor may request this during a lawsuit so that the property remains available to satisfy a judgement ordered as resolution of the suit by the court.

13. **D) Special assessment**

A special assessment tax is a tax that is levied on homeowners to fund a specific project. This tax is levied among a pre-set number of years and is then discontinued.

Practice Test 4 – Answers

14. **C) Servient estate**

A servient estate is the land that has been burdened by an easement while a dominant estate is the land that has been benefited by the easement.

15. **B) Assessment**

An assessment is not a type of easement. Appurtenant, by prescription, by necessity and in gross are all types of easements.

16. **C) Deed restrictions**

This is a limitation on how property can be used. This can limit what is done on the property and how an owner can build on property.

17. **B) Survivorship**

This is the right of co-owners to automatically receive a deceased co-owner's title of property immediately without probate.

18. **A) Subjacent support**

This means that a property's support of the surface is through the underlying strata of the earth. It is also defined as the right of the land to be supported by the land which lies under it.

19. **C) To establish priority of real property ownership interests between individuals with competing claims**

Recording establishes procedures for individuals to file copies of real property documents such as deeds, liens, and mortgages.

20. **C) Severalty**

This occurs when a property or land is owned by a single person and provides the owner with the most complete control of the land.

21. **A) Riparian rights**

Riparian rights is a system of allocating water among those who possess land along its path. This includes access to and use of the water.

22. **A) Hypothecation**

This is when real property is used as collateral to secure a debt. In this case the borrower normally has possession of property.

23. **B) Reversionary interest**

This is the interest a person has in a property when a preceding estate ceases to exist. Any interest in enjoyment of which is postponed.

24. **D) All of the above**

All of the above are examples of unilateral contracts. This is an agreement that the offeror promises to pay after the occurrence of a specified act.

25. **A) Friendly foreclosure**

This type of foreclosure entails an agreement between the borrower, senior lender, and a buyer to which the lender will foreclose its liens and transfer its collateral to the buyer with the cooperation of management.

26. **B) The veterans affairs**

The veterans affairs or the authorized agent must give approval to assume a mortgage. An assumable mortgage is one that can be taken over from the seller, by the buyer with little to no changes in terms.

27. **B) Abstract of title**

This is the condensed history of a title to a particular parcel of real estate. It consists of a summary of the original grant and all subsequent conveyances and encumbrances that affect the property. It also has a certificate by the abstractor that the history is complete and accurate.

28. **C) Acceleration clause**

This clause can be enforced if the lender chooses to if the borrower defaults on payments on a mortgage or a deed.

29. **A) In writing**

Acceptance is required to be in writing if it is pertaining to real property. It also must be communicated to the opposite party to create a contract.

30. **D) Accretion**

This is the increase of land from soil accumulation from any body of water, such as a lake, stream, or the ocean.

31. **C) When a landlord fails to provide the necessary services**

In this type of eviction, the tenant is legally entitled to cancel the lease because the landlord fails to provide the necessary services.

32. **D) All of the above**

Adverse notorious possession is also needed to claim adverse possession.

33. **B) Aesthetic zoning**

In this type of zoning, regulations are for things such as the architectural and landscaping. This is done to preserve the aesthetic features of an area.

34. **A) Agency**

An agency occurs between a principal and an agent who agree that the agent is authorized to represent the principal in specific transactions.

35. **B) Alienation clause**

This clause prevents a borrower from allowing someone else to assume debt without the lender's approval.

36. **D) Addendum**

This is an additional document that gets added to the purchase and sale agreement. This document includes any information or requests that the buyer did not put into the original purchase and sale agreement.

37. **C) Annexation**

This is the addition to property by attaching a smaller item to the larger property. The term is usually used to signify connecting a smaller item to a larger one.

38. **A) Actual eviction**

This is the legal process which will result in a tenant being physically removed from the leased premises.

39. **D) Action to quiet title**

This is lawsuit brought to court to establish a party's title to real property and to quiet claims or challenges against a title.

40.   **B) Avulsion**

This occurs when there is removal of land from a bank or shoreline. It is a sudden removal of land and the land will still remain the property of the original owner.

Resources

3.1 Finding a broker

Now that you've passed the exam, it's time to officially become an agent! Below is a list of companies and their websites to help you expedite your job search and help you start your journey in selling your first property!

Allen Tate Realtors – http://www.allentate.com/
Beacon Title Agency – http://www.beacontitle.com/
Bell Partners Inc. – http://www.bellpartnersinc.com/
Beverly-Hanks – https://www.beverly-hanks.com/
Divaris Real Estate – http://www.divaris.com/
Faison Enterprises – http://www.faison.com/
Hatteras Realty – https://www.hatterasrealty.com/
Helen Adams Realty – https://www.helenadamsrealty.com/
Home Team – http://www.hometeamsales.com/
Jim Buff Real Estate – https://jimbuff.com/
Koury – http://www.kourycorp.com/
Landmark Realty Group – https://www.landmarkrg.com/
Legacy Real Estate Advisors – https://www.legacycre.com/
MPV Properties – http://www.mpvre.com/
NAI Southern Real Estate – http://www.srenc.com/

Select Homes – https://selecthomestn.com/
Sterling – https://sterlingrealestatepartners.com/
Tanger Factory Outlet Centers – https://www.tangeroutlet.com/mebane
Ted Abbott - Mathers Realty – http://www.mathersrealty.com/
Trinity Partners – https://www.trinity-partners.com/

3.2 Interviewing

Congratulations! You did get the interview. Now, just a little work and you can ace it!

First, start by going to all of the social media pages associated with your potential employer. Focus on several interesting things that they do and specialize in. Look at which type of listings they are showing on their pages and what types of neighborhoods they appear for listings. Look up the particular broker you are interviewing with and go to his/her LinkedIn page and learn more about her/him.

While you're looking at your potential employer's social media pages, take a look at your own. Are there any posts on your Facebook or other social media sites that need to be removed? Employers are looking at your pages. Anything inappropriate needs to go!

Real estate is all about creating a network of potential clients who trust that what you're selling to them will meet their needs. This means you must understand to differentiate between a client looking to buy a house to raise their newborn and a client who is looking for long term appreciation.

Try simulating cold calls by opening up random properties on Zillow or Trulia, studying them for 2 minutes, and then trying to sell your friend on these properties. They will most likely be asking similar questions to actual prospective buyers or sellers, so it's a very useful exercise in preparing yourself for the mock cold call during the interview.

In addition, study the geography of your broker's city to make sure you don't go in completely blind. Get familiar with the prices and trends in those areas and even take a tour. Drive or walk around and know the neighborhood like the back of your hand so you can impress the employer

On the day of the interview choose your outfit carefully. You should wear some type of suit and make sure your shoes are in good condition. Ask a friend to give you input on the clothes that make you look the most professional. Make sure you brushed your teeth, and your hair is neatly styled. Make sure you don't smell of smoke as most workplaces are smoke-free. No perfume or cologne – your new office may be perfume free. Never chew gum! You will not get the job!

When you arrive at the interview, always make sure to greet the receptionist. Every person you meet at your potential future employer is important! Make a good impression.

When you land the interview, it's important to have certain answers prepared to more commonly asked questions. First, let's look at general types of questions that you may be asked at any type of interview:

1. Tell me about yourself. This is not the time to talk about everything that happened to you from birth. This is an opportunity to show off a certain drive or characteristic or hobby that is special and helps to explain why you are seeking that particular job. For example, did you participate in a lot of team sports or a lot of clubs in high school or college? Did you work on volunteer projects that required you to meet a lot of new people of all ages and work with them and/or help them? The interviewer has your resume (Always bring extras with you!), so you do not have to spout off all of your previous education and positions. Devote just a sentence or two to that part of your answer.

2. What are your greatest strengths and weaknesses? This is a very tricky question. We all know our strengths; winning personality, gets along with everyone, good at math, good at negotiating, etc., but what about our weaknesses? Well, you certainly want to be honest but now isn't the time to confess all. Choose one. Do you take too long sometimes on a project because you want every detail to be perfect? Do you sometimes want to do something completely by yourself, but you really would be better off asking others for help? These are just two examples of weaknesses that won't sound like you are unprepared for your new job.

3. Where do you see yourself in 5 years? This seems pretty straightforward but be careful. The person interviewing you could be a manager. It is best not to say that you want his/her job. Instead, it may be better to say, I see myself expanding into new roles, doing what I do better, expanding my client base, becoming more successful, continuing my real estate education, and similar phrases.

4. Why did you choose our Company? Everyone asks this question. If you haven't gone to the Company's website, don't go to the interview. You should know everything about the Company and the local office where you are interviewing. You should know which type of real estate they specialize in, how long it's been in business, any recent mergers or expansions, the physical area it is licensed to practice in, and as much as you find on their website and Facebook page and other social media.

5. Why should I hire you and not the next person? This is your moment in the spotlight. Don't just say "pick me!!". Here is a sample: "All of my life, I have enjoyed working with people; when I worked at X company or volunteered at Y organization, I was able to get along with all types of people from children to the elderly. I also have been on teams or worked on teams, and I enjoy it greatly. I like to help people, and there is no bigger purchase than a home. I believe that I have the people skills and the real estate knowledge that I need to be a successful addition to your Company.

6. Why are you leaving your current job? This is not the moment to say how much you dislike your current manager or co-worker. Always be positive at your interview. You can talk about the lack of advancement opportunities, a salary freeze, future layoff being expected, change in your current employer's office location, or some other concrete reason. You can even say that you don't feel all of your skills are being utilized, and you want to use your new knowledge every day in your job.

7. Give me an example of a situation where you used teamwork to accomplish your goal. Even if you only work by yourself at your current job, look back to previous jobs and have the answer

ready. If you don't have a job that matches, think about your volunteer activities at your children's school or at a community center or retirement village.

8. Would you rather work by yourself or as part of a team? This may be a good one to answer with a bit of vagueness. You can say that it depends on what the assignment might be. Do you have to give a major presentation to a commercial client? That might be a great time to ask for input and help as needed. Do you have to write a simple analysis of a problem? Maybe you feel more comfortable completing this on your own. You might want to say that it is very important to ask for feedback from co-workers and managers on projects and on small assignments when you have questions or reach a dead end.

9. What type of manager do you prefer? Do you prefer to work independently or to have more direction? This is always a tricky one as well. Make sure, once again, that you don't diss any of your former managers. A good response would be that you expect some direction from your manager. You feel that you know generally when you need help and would be sure to ask your manager for direction at those times. Also, you welcome all constructive feedback. It is very important to show that you are open to learning and open to change.

10. Why do you have gaps on your resume? Make sure you know the answer in advance to this question. Were you raising a family, taking care of an elderly parent, moving across the country due to a partner relocation, volunteering, etc.? Whatever it is, make sure to answer this one without any hesitation and move on.

11. What is customer service? Be careful with this one. There are two types of customers – internal and external. Everyone you work with in your office is an internal customer; others are external. The same level of consideration should be given to both internal and external customers. Speak about how important it is to answer questions, do tasks that are needed, go above and beyond the average effort, and ask for help if you don't know the answers.

12. Are you organized? No one wants to admit they are disorganized. If you are going into real estate where there are mounds of paperwork and so many different elements to keep track with, let's assume that every person interviewing for this position must be organized!

13. What do you do when several people give you tasks to do, and it is clear to you that you will not be able to finish them on time?

14. Tell me about a time when you went above and beyond what was required? Hopefully, this will be an easy one to answer. Think about a suggestion you made to your manager to take on more work when a fellow employee was out sick or a time when you thought the presentation needed a special PowerPoint and you produced it.

15. Tell me about a time you had to deal with a difficult person and how you managed to diffuse the situation? You really need to think about this one in advance. If you can't think of a difficult person in your professional life, think about a friend of a friend or someone else. Always acknowledge a difficult person's feelings and avoid arguing about strong opinions that impact an issue that isn't really that important.

16. If we offer you the position, how much notice do you have to give to your current employer? Be prepared to know the answer to this one. If you say that you can leave tomorrow, your future employer may not be pleased. It shows that you are not being loyal to your current employer by leaving them in the lurch. Two weeks is standard practice, but if you have a contract, be sure to read it.

Then, you will be asked more specific questions that are relevant to the real estate industry or this particular job. These include but are not limited to:

1. Why do you want to work in the real estate business?
2. This is a commission-based business, which means there is no ceiling to how much you can earn, but it also means there is no floor either. Are you open to this?
3. Let's go through a mock cold call together. I'll be the buyer, and you'll be the seller's agent.
4. How would you sell a property in a neighborhood you've never been to before?
5. A couple is looking to buy their first home. What kind of houses would you suggest?
6. A seasoned investor is looking for investment properties. By coincidence, the Independence Hall is for sale and you are the seller's agent. Pitch it to them.
7. A retiree is looking to sell their house. He is unsure about whether it's a good time to sell it. Explain to them why it is a good time to put the property on the market.

Be prepared to answer technical questions you may have studied for your exam such as:

1. What is the difference between a joint tenancy and a tenancy by the entireties?
2. What is the difference between a cooperative and a condominium?
3. Why is title insurance important?
4. Why would a buyer agree to lease back to a seller?
5. What are the duties of a buyer's agent?
6. What is a tax credit opposed to a tax deduction?
7. What is an easement?
8. Why would someone want to partition property, and what does this mean?
9. When would there be a lien on real estate?
10. What happens at settlement?
11. Why would a homeowner agree to finance a second mortgage for the buyer?

At the end of an interview, the interviewer will always ask if you have any questions. It is never a good idea to say, "No"! Here are some suggestions:

1. If I work here full time, what would be a range of the commissions I could expect in the first year?
2. What type of commission structure is there? Are commissions paid immediately upon closing? What types of fees am I required to pay out-of-pocket? Do I pay any advertising, computer, or other fees?
3. How often would I normally be assigned floor duty? If I answer the phone while on floor duty, do I get that listing?
4. How many open houses would I normally attend a month?
5. What is your hiring process timewise?
6. Do you pay for continuing education?

7. Although I know there isn't a truly "typical" day, what kinds of activities will I be performing during my first few weeks on the job?
8. When I attend my first settlement, will someone more senior come with me to the closing?
9. Will I attend all of the inspections for my listings?
10. What are the types of problems that arise at settlement?
11. Do you give out a list of mortgage brokers to clients?
12. How many people work in this office?
13. Is there coordination with other nearby offices – both this brand and others?
14. Do you provide a list of mortgage brokers to the buyer?

When you are finished with your interview, make sure to thank the interviewer, ask for her/his card, and thank the receptionist before you leave. Every impression counts! When you arrive home, if you really do want to work at that office, within 24 hours write a short email thank you note to your interviewer. If you don't hear back within a week, you can send a brief follow-up e-mail expressing your continuing interest in the position.